Tapestry of Loss

A FAMILY'S PATH TO
HEALING AND HOPE

KATHY AND PETER GEORGE

ISBN: 978-1-968061-44-9

Dedication

To our children,

Parenting through loss has been our most challenging yet most rewarding role. You are the reason we pursue each day with courage and hope. Watching you grow, overcome, and find your paths in life is our greatest joy. Your resilience and strength inspire us, and in you, we find the unwavering spirit of love and perseverance. This book is a testament to our journey together – a journey of pain, healing, and unending love. May it remind us of our unbreakable bond and the light you bring into our lives, even in the darkest times.

To the brave souls navigating the turbulent seas of grief,

You embody courage and resilience in the face of overwhelming loss. Your journey, marked by sorrow and strength, deeply inspires each word written on these pages. In sharing our experiences, we hope to offer you comfort, empathy, and a beacon of hope during times of profound challenge. Within these chapters, may you find solace and see a reflection of your indomitable spirit. Know that your journey is not one walked alone; together, we tread the path of healing and rediscovery, finding new meaning and moments of joy in the wake of loss.

Thank you to those who encouraged us to write; you know who you are. Your faith in our voice turned whispers of thought into the reality of these pages. This book is a tribute to belief in the power of shared stories and healing words.

Dear Reader,

If you are holding this book, it is likely that grief has touched your life in some way. First and foremost, we want to say: you are not alone.

This book is born from the deepest parts of our hearts and our personal experience with loss. When we lost our son, our lives were forever changed. Grief brought with it profound pain, questions we couldn't answer, and a sense of isolation we never imagined. But through this journey, we also discovered something unexpected: the transformative power of resilience, love, and hope.

"Tapestry of Loss" is our story, but it is also so much more. It is a guide, a companion, and a source of understanding for anyone navigating the uncertain terrain of grief. Here, we share not only our experiences but also practical tools and insights drawn from Kathy's work as a grief coach and our shared journey as a family.

This book is for you—the person searching for comfort in the chaos, meaning in the loss, and a light to guide you forward. It's for anyone yearning to honor their grief while rediscovering hope.

Thank you for allowing us to share this journey with you. We hope this book serves as a reminder that, even in the darkest moments, healing and joy are possible.

With love and compassion,
Kathy and Peter George

Table of Contents

Introduction 7

Chapter 1: Supporting Others in Grief: Empathetic Connection and Compassion 17

Chapter 2: Your Emotional Toolkit 24

Chapter 3: The Day We All Changed Forever 43

Chapter 4: A Stranger in My Own Life: Navigating Loss and Rebuilding Identity 47

Chapter 5: Navigating the Haze: The First Few Months 54

Chapter 6: Healing the Nervous System: A Symphony of Self-Care .. 64

Chapter 7: United in Grief: Supporting Each Other & Strengthening Our Marriage Through Loss 75

Chapter 8: Grief Brain, Memory & Cognitions: Navigating the Mental Landscape 84

Chapter 9: Evolution of Parenting in the Shadow of Loss 92

Chapter 10: Navigating Social Currents and Keeping My Radar Clean in a World of Hurt 104

Chapter 11: Compassion Unleashed: Navigating Self-Compassion and Forgiveness for Others 115

Chapter 12: Navigating Anger, Guilt, and Regret in Grief's Dance 125

Chapter 13: Rediscovering Joy: Whatever Makes Your Heart Beat Again 135

Chapter 14: Navigating the Calendar: Holidays, Anniversaries, Birthdays 144

Chapter 15: Sacred Spaces: His Room and Belongings 155

Chapter 16: Embracing Change: Redefining Normal 163

Chapter 17: Navigating Grief's Isolation and
Relationship Changes 172

Chapter 18: The Weight of Expectations: Societal and
Self-Imposed... 191

Chapter 19: The Fear of Forgetting: Preserving Memories.............. 199

Chapter 20: Faith and Spirituality: Navigating the
Spiritual Landscape... 208

Chapter 21: The Lingering Questions: Finding Answers and
Acceptance in Our Journey 216

Chapter 22: Transformative Energies of Grief and Unexpected
Blessings Found Along the Way 224

Chapter 23: The Beacon of Hope: Navigating Forward.................. 231

In Closing 242

Bibliography 244

About the Authors...252

Introduction

"Although the world is full of suffering, it is also full of the overcoming of it." —Helen Keller

First and foremost, if you're turning these pages in the wake of profound loss, please accept my deepest condolences. You're not alone on this journey. Peter and I hope these pages offer you connection, insight, and a shared sense of empathy. While your grief journey is deeply personal and unique, the universal thread of loss connects us all, reminding us that we're not alone. May today bring you moments of kindness and solace.

Our journey through loss began in August of 2014. In the immediate aftermath of our loss, there was a flurry of condolences, meals, and sympathetic gestures. Friends, family, and even acquaintances rallied around us, offering their support in various forms. We were and continue to be grateful for the support that carried us through those first weeks. However, as the weeks passed, this initial wave of support began to recede. The phone calls became less frequent, the visits dwindled, and gradually, we faced overwhelming silence. A sense of isolation set in as we grappled with the stark contrast between the initial outpouring of care and the ensuing silence. This lack of ongoing support left us in a vulnerable state. This sudden shift exacerbated the sense of loneliness, leaving us to navigate the complexities of grief largely alone. The world seemed to move on, but for us, time stood still. We were navigating an unfamiliar terrain of sorrow and longing, yet the resources and comprehension we desperately needed seemed scarce. It wasn't just the absence of physical support that was striking; it was also the lack of insight about the enduring nature of grief. The prevailing expectation seemed to be that we would, or should, start to "move past" our loss after a socially acceptable period of mourning.

The realization that grief is a misunderstood and neglected aspect of our society became increasingly apparent. Support systems, both formal and informal, seemed ill-equipped to handle the long-term, fluctuating nature of grief. We encountered a lack of spaces where our grief could be expressed and understood without judgment, a lack of resources that addressed the ongoing challenges of living with loss, and general discomfort in society when it came to discussing and dealing with grief. This experience highlighted a significant gap in societal attitudes toward grief and bereavement. It underscored the need for more sustained, informed, and compassionate support systems that recognize grief as a long-term journey, not a short-term condition to be swiftly overcome. Our journey through loss was not just a personal journey of mourning; it was also a wake-up call about the societal changes needed to support grieving families better.

The profound impact of loss extends well beyond emotional pain to almost every facet of life and our existence. I was acutely aware of its impact across my life, from home to work, to my sleep, to my most basic needs. Daily tasks, once performed almost mindlessly, became burdensome, each a reminder of the gaping hole left in our family. Even simple acts like setting the table or doing laundry became laden with sorrow as I was constantly reminded of the one who was missing. Even basic needs, like sleep, eating, and self-care, were impacted. The pleasure and comfort once found in food and hobbies dissipated. Meals became mechanical acts of sustenance rather than moments of family togetherness or culinary enjoyment. Activities that used to bring joy or relaxation lost their appeal, leaving me listless and disconnected.

Possible Health Implications of Grief

What I wasn't aware of, though, was the possible health implications of grief, as it can aggravate existing conditions and potentially cause new ones. The Harvard Health Blog (n.d.) underscores the stress grief places on the body, notably on organ systems like the immune system. This stress can weaken immune cell function and increase inflammatory responses, heightening illness susceptibility and healthcare needs. Moreover, stress, an everyday companion of grief, triggers the release of stress hormones, adversely affecting existing health conditions and potentially giving rise to new ones. Conditions such as heart failure, diabetes, high blood pressure, heartburn, insomnia, and changes in appetite can be exacerbated or initiated by stress (Harvard Health Publishing, n.d.).

Between the lack of support and our not knowing the impact of grief on health, we didn't do much to attend to our grief for at least four years. Keeping the kids in service was our focus. As a result, Peter and I were not adequately addressing our emotional and mental well-being, inadvertently putting our needs on the back burner as we navigated this uncharted territory. Echoing Robert Bly's words, "The body weeps the tears the eyes never shed," we see the profound impact of unexpressed grief. When I was finally aware of the profound and multifaceted impact grief had on our lives, it led me down a path of deep personal and professional transformation. Pursuing a master's degree in mental health counseling was a step borne out of necessity – a response to the void that our loss had created and the subsequent realization of how under-addressed grief is in our society. This educational pursuit was about more than acquiring academic credentials; it was an endeavor to deeply understand the psychological underpinnings of grief, explore therapeutic approaches, and learn how to support others grappling with similar experiences effectively.

At this point, we had already navigated significant health issues with Peter. Unbeknownst to me at the time, my health was also heading towards a similar trajectory, a silent testament to the often-overlooked physical toll of intense, unattended, prolonged grief. The dawning awareness that our emotional well-being had been largely overlooked in the wake of our loss was a pivotal moment. It steered me towards a decision that would reshape my professional identity and offer a new avenue for healing. The journey through this program was transformative. It gave me a profound insight into the complexities of human emotions, the spirit's resilience, and the therapeutic process. I was not just learning theories and counseling techniques; I was also learning about myself, about the depths of my grief, and about the healing power of offering support to others. This newfound knowledge and perspective brought a sense of clarity and purpose. As I delved deeper into my studies, I saw where Peter and I had struggled without adequate support. I understood the importance of addressing each facet of grief – emotional, mental, physical, and even spiritual. This holistic approach became a cornerstone of my healing journey and professional coaching practice. By the time I received my diagnosis, I was acutely aware of the crucial link between physical, mental, and spiritual well-being. Recognizing this interconnectedness, I knew what steps I needed to take – not just for the benefit of others, as had been my focus, but for myself this time. I took time to proceed through treatment, allowing myself the space to recover both mentally and physically. During this period, I focused on nurturing my well-being, embracing practices that supported my mental health, engaging in activities that fostered physical healing, and seeking experiences that nourished my spirit.

Profound loss, like the death of a loved one, significantly impacts physical health, often triggering stress-related changes in the immune system and exacerbating or even causing various health conditions (Ader & Cohen, 1993). Acknowledging and addressing this complex relationship between grief and physical well-being is crucial. We hope this book offers practical strategies to navigate this stress effectively, lessening its impact on physical health. It provides tools for building emotional resilience, becoming an invaluable resource for those experiencing the physical effects of loss. Actively processing grief is vital, allowing the release of pent-up emotions and preventing their manifestation as physical symptoms. This process of emotional release is more than just healing; it's a recognition of the depth of our grief, intertwining our emotional and physical health on the path to recovery (Ader & Cohen, 1993).

Relationships Under the Strain of Grief

Adding to these challenges is the documented research on how profound loss can strain relationships, potentially leading to increased marital difficulties or even divorce. A study published in the U.S. National Library of Medicine (Parkes, 1998) revealed that the death of a child is a traumatic event with enduring effects on parents' lives. Research on bereaved parents, as noted by Rogers et al. (2008), indicates increased depressive symptoms, poorer well-being, and other health issues, potentially leading to marital separation. The months following the loss prove emotionally, physically, and mentally taxing, often becoming the breeding ground for marital problems. According to The Center for Complicated Grief (2018) at Columbia University, parents may develop negative feelings towards their spouse post-loss, leading to withdrawal and an inability to support each other. Pre-existing marital problems can escalate, intensifying the strain. Grieving couples may grapple with blame, guilt, anger, resentment, depression, and feelings of isolation.

In our journey of grief, we faced many challenges, not least of which was the strain it placed on our relationship. During a session at a family grief support group, we encountered a startling statistic: the odds of a couple surviving the intense grief of loss was only about 50%. This information was both alarming and eye-opening for us.

This statistic, often cited in discussions about grief and relationships, suggests a significant risk of marital strain or dissolution following the intense loss. While the exact source of this figure is difficult to pinpoint, it is commonly referenced in grief counseling and support literature. For instance, a study by Lynda Cheldelin Fell and Dr. Gloria Horsley in their work on grief and family dynamics echoes this sentiment, highlighting the profound impact the loss of a child can have on a marriage (Fell, Beltz, Elizabeth, Martin, Rollins, & Kelly, 2015).

For us, this revelation was a wake-up call. It underscored the need for open communication and mutual support as we navigated our grief journey. We realized that while our individual experiences of grief might differ, it was crucial for our relationship's survival to understand and respect each other's coping mechanisms.

This statistic also prompted us to seek additional support as individuals, as a couple, and as a family. We understood that we needed to work on our relationship actively to avoid becoming part of this statistic. This involved regular check-ins with each other and joining support groups where we could learn from and lean on other couples facing similar challenges.

In essence, being informed about the potential risks to our relationship in the face of grief guided us to take proactive steps to strengthen our bond. It encouraged us to face our grief together, maintaining a united front even in the depths of our sorrow.

Comprehending Secondary Losses

The concept of "secondary losses" in grief refers to the additional losses that occur as a direct or indirect result of the primary loss. These are often not immediately apparent but become more evident and impactful over time. In the context of losing a child like Trevor, the primary loss is the death of the child. However, this event can lead to a cascade of secondary losses, each compounding the grief experience. Here's an explanation of how these secondary losses can hit even harder:

Loss of Identity: Parents often define themselves in relation to their children. With the loss of a child, there's a profound impact on one's sense of identity. You may no longer see yourself as that child's parent in the physical world, leading to a deep existential crisis.

Changed Family Dynamics: The loss of a child can drastically alter the family structure and dynamics. Relationships with other children or your partner may change, sometimes leading to emotional distance or conflict, as each person copes with the loss differently.

Loss of Future: The death of a child brings the loss of the future you envisioned with them. Milestones such as birthdays, graduations, weddings, and even the simple everyday moments you expected to share are now a source of pain. Each one hits, and some repeat every year.

Social and Community Changes: Relationships with friends and community may change. You might find yourself disconnected from previous social circles, either because others are unsure how to support you or because you no longer feel a sense of belonging due to your grief.

Impact on Personal Beliefs and Worldview: There can be a profound impact on your beliefs and perception of the world. This might include questioning religious beliefs, the fairness of life, or your previously held values and priorities.

Emotional and Psychological Impact: Besides the immediate grief, there can be long-term emotional and psychological effects, such as depression, anxiety, or post-traumatic stress disorder.

Physical Health Changes: Grief can take a toll on physical health. The stress and emotional turmoil might lead to sleep disturbances, changes in appetite, or other health issues.

Secondary losses are often more complicated to cope with because they are less tangible and more pervasive than the primary loss. They permeate multiple aspects of life, sometimes unexpectedly, and can prolong or complicate the grieving process. Recognizing and addressing these secondary losses is crucial in the journey towards healing and adaptation.

How to Use This Book

As we share our journey nine years following the sudden, unexplained passing of our son Trevor, we hope that you can navigate this book seamlessly and utilize the suggestions and support sections to mitigate health impacts and relationship struggles. This book is a guide crafted for those journeying through the difficult terrain of grief, intertwining our shared experiences with research-driven insights and practical advice from my personal journey and professional expertise as a grief coach. A common theme throughout this book is the importance of giving yourself grace. It embodies the epitome of self-compassion. Treating oneself with kindness and patience is a comforting and supportive beacon and fosters an environment conducive to growth and resilience. We hope this book will be your compassionate companion, offering solace, insight, and a roadmap for healing on your unique grief journey.

We have intentionally incorporated some repetition across the chapters, as we envision each chapter should stand independently, providing sufficient information and support. This design choice recognizes that grievers may have limited time and capacity for reading, allowing them to quickly access the support and empathy they need without the burden of reading the entire book or following a sequential order. By doing so, we aim to deliver empathetic and accessible content that respects those navigating through grief's unique needs and circumstances.

This journey began with the unimaginable loss of Trevor. Through sharing this deeply personal experience, we've opened a window into the complexities of grief and how it reshapes our lives through the primary loss and the secondary losses. Throughout this book, we will touch on the initial shock, the overwhelming emotions, and the disorientation accompanying such a significant loss. It is more than just a narrative of sorrow. It's a testament to the strength of the human spirit in the face of adversity. We hope it serves as a reminder that, even in our darkest hours, we are not alone in our experiences. The stories and reflections shared here aim to provide comfort, insight, and a sense of solidarity to anyone walking this challenging path.

As you turn the page, remember that grief is a journey that unfolds in its own time and in its own way. The emotions and experiences shared are the beginning of a longer process of healing and growth. The path ahead may be uncertain and, at times, challenging. Still, it is also a path that can lead to deeper insight, resilience, and a renewed appreciation for life's precious moments.

If you are looking to support others in grief, a few great chapters to start with include Chapter 1, "Supporting Others in Grief: Empathetic Connection and Compassion," which clarifies how to prioritize support in the first days of loss; Chapter 10, "Navigating Social Currents and Keeping My Radar Clean in a World of Hurt," offering insights into the daily experience of grief through its lens; and Chapter 17, "Navigating Grief's Isolation and Relationship Changes," guiding what to say and how to address shifts in social dynamics.

CHAPTER 1

Supporting Others in Grief: Empathetic Connection and Compassion

"The most compassionate thing we can do for those in grief is to be willing to stand quietly beside them in their darkness." —Unknown

As you embark on reading *Tapestry of Loss*, I want to draw your attention to the unique format of this opening chapter. Unlike the subsequent chapters, which delve deeply into various aspects of grief and healing for those in grief, this first chapter is intentionally structured to be a quick and accessible read for those supporting someone in grief. The aim is to provide immediate, actionable support in a format that can be easily understood and applied, even amid challenging times.

In my journey through grief, I've learned that supporting others who are mourning is a delicate yet profoundly important task. The way we offer support can be a source of comfort or unintentional distress. This chapter aims to guide you through providing support with empathy and compassion.

One of the most effective frameworks I've encountered in this regard is the Ring Theory of grief support, developed by clinical psychologist Susan Silk and her friend Barry Goldman. This theory, also known as the "Circle of Support," offers a clear and compassionate guideline for providing support during times of crisis (Silk & Goldman, 2013).

The Ring Theory is visualized as a series of concentric circles. At the center of these circles is the person most directly affected by the loss – in the context of grief, this would typically be the deceased's immediate family members. The central principle of the Ring Theory is "Comfort In, Dump Out." This means that comfort should always flow towards the center, towards those most affected by the loss, while any venting or processing of one's own emotions about the crisis should be directed outwards, towards those less affected or those in one's support network (Armstrong, n.d.; Sandler, 2017).

In practical terms, the person at the center of the ring can express their feelings without filter – they can freely express sadness, frustration, or confusion. Those in the circles immediately surrounding them – close friends and extended family – are there to provide support and comfort, listening and offering help without burdening the central person with their grief or reactions. For those further out, including colleagues and acquaintances, their role is to support those in the inner rings and find their support externally if needed. This approach helps ensure that the bereaved, who are dealing with the most intense aspects of grief, are not burdened further by the emotional needs of others.

The individuals at the circle's center do not have the resources to carry anyone else's losses. They are tending to the trauma of the loss, and that alone will consume their every resource. This is where people can shift whether they are a source of support or a source of distress for the ones in grief. It is not a time to compare the amount of grief and or their reaction to the loss. For those of us who find ourselves in one of the outer circles, it's important to remember that while our feelings of grief and loss are valid, our primary role in the situation is to offer support and comfort to those more directly affected by the loss (Daily Shoring, n.d.).

Ring Theory is a valuable tool in the realm of grief support. It offers a compassionate and structured method for providing support, ensuring that the needs of the bereaved are prioritized and that the support offered by others is appropriate and respectful of their situation.

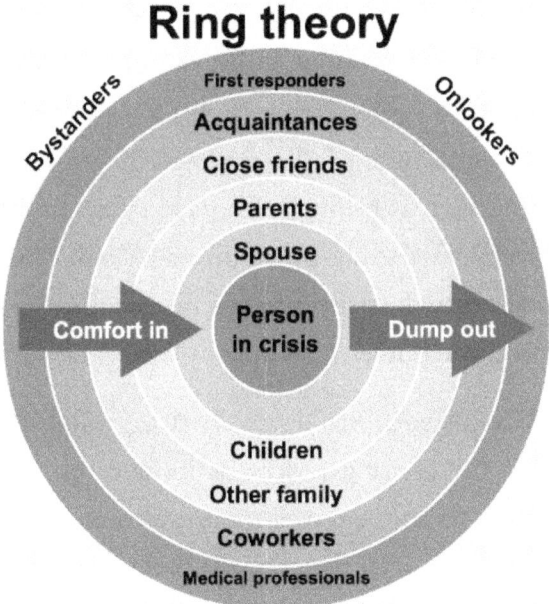

Moving beyond the structured approach of Ring Theory, let's explore other general strategies that can equally effectively support those in grief.

Listen Actively: One of the most valuable things you can do is to listen. Allow them to express their feelings without judgment or the need to offer solutions. Active listening involves being fully present, acknowledging their feelings, and showing empathy.

Active listening plays a critical role in providing support. It involves fully concentrating, comprehending, responding, and remembering what is said (Rogers & Farson, 1957). This empathetic form of listening validates their feelings and helps them feel heard and acknowledged (Rogers & Farson, 1957).

Acknowledge Their Loss: Recognize the loss and its impact on their life. Simple expressions of sympathy, like "I'm sorry for your loss," can be meaningful. Avoid trying to downplay the loss or resort to clichés that might minimize their pain.

Offer Practical Help: Sometimes, the best support is practical assistance. This could include helping with daily chores, providing meals, or assisting with funeral arrangements. Offering specific help is often more helpful than a general offer of "let me know if you need anything." Practical support, such as helping with daily tasks, can be immensely helpful. According to a study by Smith and Cook (2019), practical assistance can alleviate the daily stressors that compound the grieving individual's emotional burden.

Be Patient and Consistent: Grief doesn't have a timeline. Be patient and understand that the grieving process is unique to each individual. Continue to check in on them over time, even after the initial loss, as grief can resurface long after the event. It's essential to be patient and consistent in your support. What the bereaved needs can change over time; being a steady presence ready to offer support is invaluable (Kübler-Ross & Kessler, 2005).

Respect Their Way of Grieving: People grieve differently. It is essential to recognize that the grieving process is deeply personal and manifests differently for everyone. While some individuals find solace in sharing their stories and emotions, others may seek comfort in quiet reflection or immerse themselves in activities. Honoring their preferred way of coping, be it through conversation or contemplation, is a fundamental aspect of support. Please give them the freedom to navigate their journey, recognizing that their needs may change along the way, with fluctuating levels of tolerance, energy, and emotional bandwidth.

Avoid Clichés and Easy Answers: Phrases like "They're in a better place now" or "Everything happens for a reason" can often feel dismissive. It's better to acknowledge the difficulty of the situation than to try to explain it away.

Remember Significant Dates: Supporting someone in grief during significant dates and holidays can be particularly challenging, as these times often heighten feelings of loss and loneliness. Birthdays, anniversaries, and holidays, traditionally times of joy and gathering, can underscore the absence of a loved one, intensifying the grief experience. Zisook and Shear (2009) point out that the first year of grief is often the most difficult, with holidays and anniversaries triggering intense emotions. It's essential to offer gentle support, acknowledging that the bereaved might want to alter or skip holiday traditions (Harvard Health Publishing, 2019). Encouraging the expression of feelings, whether it's sadness, anger, or a sense of loss, is crucial, as suppressing grief can lead to prolonged emotional distress (Stroebe et al., 2007). Creating new traditions that honor the memory of the deceased can also be therapeutic, fostering a sense of continuity and connection (Neimeyer, 2001). Throughout the holiday season, the best support one can offer is a compassionate presence, allowing the grieving individual to experience and express their emotions in a safe and empathetic environment. Acknowledging these dates and offering support or a listening ear can be very meaningful. Allowing for flexibility in traditions and plans can differentiate between being supportive and adding to the griever's distress.

Encourage Professional Help if Needed: When grief appears overwhelming or persistent, offering a gentle suggestion for professional counseling or grief coaching can be beneficial. Approach the topic with sensitivity, ensuring they don't feel judged or that their grief is being dismissed as atypical. It's also compassionate to acknowledge that while you may not fully grasp the depth of their loss, you recognize the importance of being heard by someone who might. Witnessing grief is a vital part of the healing process, and though society may not always show the necessary patience or empathy, remember that the priority in such moments is the well-being of the grieving, not the comfort of the supporters.

Educate Yourself About Grief: Gaining insight into the grieving process can help you be more empathetic and effective in your support. Many resources are available that explain the various stages and manifestations of grief. Recognizing the diverse ways in which people grieve is also vital. Worden (2018) notes that grief is a multifaceted response to loss, unique to each individual. This means that our support must be tailored to the specific needs and experiences of the bereaved, acknowledging that there is no "one-size-fits-all" approach to grief (Worden, 2018).

Be There, Even in Silence: The simple act of being there often offers immense comfort. Silence, shared with a compassionate presence, can be a profound and supportive gesture in itself.

A few additional chapters in this book that are helpful for supporting others are Chapter 10, "Navigating Social Currents and Keeping My Radar Clean in a World of Hurt," offering insights into the daily experience of grief through its lens, and Chapter 17, "Navigating Grief's Isolation and Relationship Changes," guiding what to say and how to address shifts in social dynamics.

In closing, supporting someone in grief requires a sensitive and caring touch. It's important to recognize that the aim is not to resolve their grief but to provide solace and accompaniment throughout their journey of mourning. Your unwavering presence, enduring patience, and heartfelt empathy are the most precious contributions you can make.

CHAPTER 2

Your Emotional Toolkit

"Emotions are necessary – even when they're uncomfortable or unwanted – because they're a part of your psyche, a part of your neural network, a part of your socialization, and a part of your humanity." —Karla McLaren

When life leads us into adversity, our response isn't solely determined by the circumstances but also by how we think about these challenges and our ability to handle our emotions. Our emotional toolbox, unique to each of us, is shaped by factors like upbringing, experiences, cultural background, and biology. While some start with a well-equipped toolbox for understanding and managing emotions, others might need to develop specific key skills.

This toolbox includes abilities such as empathy, which aids in understanding others' experiences; resilience, the strength to recover from setbacks; emotional regulation, to maintain balance in our feelings; self-awareness, to recognize and understand our emotions; and communication skills, for effectively expressing our feelings.

The beauty of our emotional toolbox is that it's not fixed but adaptable. We can always add new tools and sharpen the ones we already have. Life experiences, especially when confronting adversity, offer opportunities to enhance our emotional skills. This continuous learning process enriches our understanding of ourselves, others, and the world. It's cliché but true: we can view adversity as a chance for growth or a barrier. This perspective significantly influences how we navigate challenges, impacting our resilience and outlook on life. Viewing adversity as an opportunity opens us up to learning new skills, deepening our insights, and strengthening our emotional resilience.

Conversely, seeing it only as an opposing force can hinder our progress and lead to a stagnant mindset. The key is to realize that our thoughts and reactions in the face of adversity are powerful tools for shaping our experiences and outcomes. Recognizing this empowers us to actively enhance our emotional toolbox, improving our ability to face life's challenges with resilience and insight.

This chapter will provide insight into the nature of emotions and offer practical guidance on how to expand your emotional skills. We'll look at strategies to enhance emotional intelligence, such as developing empathy, improving self-regulation, and cultivating resilience. These skills are essential for navigating life's challenges effectively and maintaining healthy relationships.

Emotions vs. Feelings

Emotions and feelings, while often used interchangeably, have distinct meanings in psychology.

Emotions are psychological states triggered by specific stimuli (like events, thoughts, or physical sensations). Emotions are often associated with physiological changes; for example, an increased heart rate when scared or blushing when embarrassed. Emotions are considered to be more raw, instinctual, and primal and include basic feelings like happiness, sadness, anger, fear, surprise, and disgust. These are universal and are often recognized across different cultures.

Feelings are the subjective perception, experience, and interpretation of emotions. They represent the personal way we experience these emotions, influenced by our individual beliefs, memories, and thoughts. Each feeling is a unique mental association and reaction to an emotion acquired through personal experience. For example, in the same situation, one person might feel anger while another feels sadness, highlighting the personal nature of feelings. Consequently, while the underlying emotion might be fear, the specific feeling could vary widely, manifesting as panic, anxiety, or apprehension, depending on the individual's processing of that emotion.

One of the most valuable tools to understand and identify emotions and feelings is the "Feelings Wheel," developed by Dr. Gloria Willcox (1982). This wheel helps individuals articulate their feelings by breaking down complex feelings into core emotions and their nuances. The wheel is divided into sections, with core emotions at the center and related, more specific feelings branching out from these. It's a helpful tool for expanding emotional vocabulary and understanding the complexity of human emotions and feelings. The premise of the Feelings Wheel is that more complex feelings are often extensions of five core emotions. These core emotions are typically happiness, sadness, anger, fear, and disgust. The wheel helps us understand that we often perceive distinct and complex feelings as nuanced versions of these primary emotions.

For instance, feelings like joy, contentment, and love stem from the core emotion of happiness. Similarly, frustration, annoyance, and rage can be traced back to anger. The wheel visually represents these connections, showing how intricate feelings branch out from more basic ones. This structure aids in identifying and articulating feelings, making it easier to understand and communicate emotional experiences. The Feelings Wheel thus serves as a valuable tool for emotional literacy, helping individuals to recognize and process their emotions more effectively.

Using the Feelings Wheel and similar resources can aid in emotional literacy, which is identifying, understanding, and responding to emotions in oneself and others. This skill is crucial for emotional intelligence, which involves recognizing, interpreting, and responding constructively to emotions.

Emotional Bandwidth

Everyone's emotional bandwidth varies greatly, and understanding this diversity is crucial to our collective growth and learning. Practicing self-compassion for our humanness and the inherent opportunity for growth is essential in navigating our emotional landscapes. Acknowledging that we are all works in progress allows us to be more forgiving of ourselves and others. It's essential to remember that personal growth is a journey, not a destination. We are constantly evolving, adapting, and learning from our experiences.

Self-compassion involves recognizing that making mistakes, feeling overwhelmed, or struggling with emotions are natural aspects of being human. Rather than being harsh or critical towards ourselves during these times, we should offer ourselves the kindness and understanding we would extend to a good friend. This approach fosters a healthier relationship with ourselves and enhances our emotional resilience.

Moreover, embracing growth encourages a mindset of openness and curiosity. It allows us to view challenges as opportunities for development and self-discovery. By nurturing self-compassion, we create a supportive inner environment for this growth, leading to a more fulfilling and emotionally balanced life.

Emotions are pivotal in our cognition, actions, and overall well-being. Davidson (2023) emphasizes that emotions are central to brain function, affecting empathy, understanding of others, and personal well-being. He highlights the interconnection between emotion and cognition, illustrating that the brain circuits controlling emotions overlap with those involved in cognitive functions, thus blurring the line between these mental processes. Davidson (2023) notes that emotions can arise from real-world experiences and mental activities, leading to various emotional states, moods, and long-term traits. Moreover, he links the study of emotions to physical health, explaining how emotional style affects mental and physical well-being, influencing various physiological systems.

In emotional intelligence, McLaren (2010) outlines four keys to achieving what can be termed "Emotional Genius." The first key is the understanding that emotions are neither inherently negative nor positive. This perspective suggests that every emotion carries vital messages and equips individuals with the necessary skills and energy to handle various situations. Embracing this viewpoint encourages a more holistic and accepting approach to emotional experiences.

The second key involves learning to channel emotions effectively instead of merely expressing or repressing them. This key emphasizes the importance of finding constructive ways to process and utilize emotions, transforming them from raw feelings into meaningful actions or insights. Channeling emotions effectively helps avoid the pitfalls of emotional extremes, such as overreaction or emotional suppression, which can harm personal well-being and interpersonal relationships.

Understanding the nuances in emotions constitutes the third key. This involves recognizing that each emotion exists on a spectrum and can manifest with varying intensity levels. By acknowledging this complexity, individuals can develop a more refined emotional awareness, enabling them to respond more appropriately to their emotional states and those of others. This nuanced understanding fosters empathy and improves communication, allowing for a more accurate interpretation of emotional expressions.

The fourth and final key is the ability to simultaneously identify the coexistence of multiple emotions. This recognizes the multifaceted nature of human experiences, where emotions are seldom experienced in isolation. By being aware of the concurrent presence of different emotions, individuals can better understand their emotional landscape. This awareness is crucial for emotional regulation and decision-making, as it helps to discern the dominant emotions that need attention and manage conflicting feelings effectively.

These four keys form a foundation for achieving emotional mastery, allowing individuals to navigate their emotional worlds with greater skill, understanding, and effectiveness. They serve as guiding principles for developing emotional intelligence, leading to a more balanced, fulfilling, and emotionally intelligent life.

Building on this understanding, David (2016) discusses the importance of all emotions, arguing against categorizing them as solely positive or negative. He introduces the concept of emotional agility, essential for well-being and success, which involves flexible responses to thoughts and feelings and helps individuals move away from emotional rigidity, often linked to psychological issues like depression and anxiety.

To cultivate emotional agility and intelligence, Bradberry and Greaves's work highlights five key skills essential for personal and professional growth (Bradberry & Greaves, 2009). The first skill is self-awareness, which involves a deep understanding of one's emotions, strengths, and weaknesses. This skill allows individuals to recognize their emotional triggers and understand the impact of their moods on their behavior and decision-making.

The second skill is self-management, which is crucial for controlling and regulating emotions, especially in challenging situations. Effective self-management enables individuals to respond to emotional stimuli thoughtfully and constructively rather than in a reactive manner. This skill encompasses techniques like breathing exercises, creating emotion versus reason lists, and practicing mindfulness to maintain emotional balance.

Social awareness, the third skill, entails the development of empathy and understanding towards others. It involves recognizing and appropriately responding to the emotions of those around us, which is vital for healthy interpersonal relationships and effective communication.

The fourth skill is relationship management, which focuses on maintaining good relationships and effectively managing conflict. This skill is pivotal for building strong personal and professional networks and involves understanding and navigating the emotions of others, as well as one's own emotions, in social interactions.

Finally, combining personal and social competence is essential for a well-rounded approach to emotional intelligence. This integration involves applying one's understanding of emotions (personal and others) in various social contexts to manage behavior, navigate social complexities, and make positive decisions.

Incorporating these skills into daily life enhances individual emotional intelligence and builds a more empathetic and emotionally aware society. By developing these skills, individuals can improve their ability to navigate the complexities of emotional experiences, both in personal and professional settings (Bradberry & Greaves, 2009).

Nolan (2023) provides insights into the Stoic approach to emotional balance and resilience. Contrary to common misconceptions, Stoicism is not about the absence of emotions but about managing them effectively. Nolan (2023) explains that Stoicism involves understanding and managing situations beyond our control using logic and reason. This philosophy encourages reflection, learning from mistakes, and developing emotional resilience. Nolan (2023) clarifies that emotional toughness, resiliency, and grit are key aspects of Stoicism, which involves understanding and controlling emotions, especially in challenging situations, to avoid adverse reactions.

In summary, these perspectives highlight the complexity and significance of emotions in our lives. Understanding and managing emotions are crucial for cognitive processes, personal well-being, and professional success. The development of emotional agility and intelligence and the Stoic approach to emotional resilience provide valuable frameworks for navigating life's challenges.

Strategies for Growth

Strategies for Emotional Self-Awareness

Observe the Ripple Effect of Emotions: Recognize how emotions impact your interactions and decision-making. Reflect on how your emotional state influences both your personal and professional life.

Lean Into Discomfort: Confront uncomfortable feelings to gain insight and resilience. This approach helps in processing and overcoming challenging emotions.

Feel Emotions Physically: Notice the physical sensations associated with different emotions to better understand their influence on your body and mind.

Know Your Emotional Triggers: Identify specific situations or interactions that trigger emotional responses, aiding in proactive emotional management.

Read Body Language: Developing a deeper understanding of emotional intelligence includes being mindful of body language (your own and others). Observing body language can provide insights into people's true feelings and help adapt your responses and reactions appropriately (Greene, 2018).

Be Empathetic: Empathy involves putting yourself in someone else's shoes and understanding the origin of their emotions. This empathy can improve how you feel about others and yourself, enhancing your confidence and emotional intelligence (Greene, 2018).

Watch Yourself Objectively: Observe your emotional reactions as if from an outsider's perspective, aiming for a non-judgmental and compassionate viewpoint.

Be Open to Feedback: Enhancing emotional intelligence includes being open and receptive to feedback, including criticisms. Welcoming feedback is a vital step in recognizing and modifying behavioral patterns that might be detrimental or unproductive. This process of acceptance and introspection is essential in developing a higher emotional quotient. It involves seeing feedback as an opportunity for growth and improvement, rather than as a negative judgment, thereby fostering personal and professional development (Greene, 2018).

Keep an Emotional Journal: Record your emotions and what triggers them to gain insights into patterns and potential areas for growth.

Understand the Impact of Moods: Acknowledge how different moods can alter your perception of events and affect your decision-making process.

Self-Management Techniques

Practice Right Breathing: Employ breathing techniques to calm emotions, especially useful during moments of stress or anxiety.

Create Emotion vs. Reason Lists: Differentiate between your emotional impulses and rational thoughts, helping to clarify decision-making processes.

Count to Ten in Emotional Situations: Implement a brief pause in emotionally charged situations to prevent impulsive reactions.

Sleep on Decisions: Delay decision-making when emotionally charged to avoid haste and ensure rationality.

Understand Yourself Under Stress: Recognize how stress influences your emotional responses and develop strategies to cope effectively.

Smile and Laugh More: Use the power of positive expressions to elevate your mood and create a positive atmosphere around you.

Acknowledge and Apologize for Mistakes: Being gracious enough to accept and apologize for hurting others is a sign of high emotional intelligence. It leads to more positive relationships and forgiveness, as opposed to living in denial (Greene, 2018).

Set Aside Problem-Solving Time: Designate specific times for addressing challenges, reducing constant preoccupation with problems.

Control Self-Talk: Monitor your internal dialogue to ensure it is supportive and constructive, rather than critical or negative.

Visualize Success: Engage in positive visualization to enhance self-confidence and motivation.

Maintain Good Sleep Hygiene: Prioritize quality sleep to support emotional stability and overall well-being.

Focus on Freedoms Rather Than Limitations: Emphasize aspects of life you can control, rather than dwelling on constraints.

Stay Synchronized with Emotions: Maintain awareness of your emotional state to ensure alignment with your responses and actions.

Speak to Someone Not Emotionally Invested: Seek objective perspectives to gain clarity and avoid biased feedback.

Learn from Every Encounter: Approach interactions as opportunities for learning and emotional development.

Adopting these strategies can significantly enhance one's emotional self-awareness and self-management capabilities, leading to improved personal well-being and more effective interpersonal relationships.

Learn How to Channel Your Emotions

Honoring Emotions: When it comes to honoring emotions, it's important to find a balanced approach that neither diminishes nor overly elevates emotions. Avoiding extremes of despising or idealizing emotions is crucial; instead, emotions should be viewed as integral components of our humanity and evolution. Recognizing emotions as valuable tools rather than as disconnected, arbitrary forces allows for a more nuanced understanding and healthier emotional management. This perspective encourages seeing emotions as informative and essential aspects of our experiences, guiding personal growth and understanding.

The Healing Balm of Sadness: This exercise is centered on embracing the therapeutic aspects of sadness. It involves taking gentle breaths to create a slight tension in the chest, holding it briefly, and then exhaling while making small, circular movements. This method helps in processing and understanding sadness, transforming it into a healing experience.

Welcoming Happiness: This practice encourages the embodiment of happiness through physical expression. Sitting comfortably, widening the eyes, smiling as if greeting a dear friend, and stretching out the arms helps in recognizing and embracing the emotion of happiness, viewing it as a rejuvenating force in one's life.

The Instinctual Gifts of Fear: This exercise focuses on tuning into the instinctual aspects of fear. By finding a quiet place to sit or stand, leaning forward slightly, and concentrating on the faintest sounds, this practice enhances awareness and connects with the instinctual signals of fear, aiding in better understanding and utilization of this emotion.

Grounding: The "Grounding" exercise, as described in McLaren's *The Language of Emotions* (2010), is a practice aimed at connecting the individual with the earth to enhance emotional stability and presence. The exercise begins with the individual finding a comfortable position for sitting or standing and engaging in gentle breathing. This step is crucial for achieving a state of relaxation and grounding, which forms the foundation of the exercise.

Participants are then guided to engage with the emotions of sadness and fear in a way that aids in focusing and grounding. They visualize warmth and light in the belly, which symbolizes the gathering of emotional energy. As they breathe out, they imagine this light and warmth moving down through the body and into the ground. This visualization helps create a mental connection between the body and the earth, symbolizing the grounding of emotional energy.

The practice also involves imagining a grounding cord extending from the body down to the earth's center. Participants are encouraged to anchor this cord in a way that resonates with them, such as visualizing it as the roots of a tree or a chain with an anchor. This imagery helps deepen the sense of connection and stability.

Throughout the exercise, individuals maintain a gentle focus on their breathing and the grounding sensation. The practice can be enhanced by slight movements or imagining the grounding cord moving with them as they walk around. This adaptability of the grounding cord symbolizes the continuous presence and support of this grounding connection in daily life.

McLaren (2010) emphasizes that grounding is a versatile and beneficial practice that can help individuals release tension, stay present, and integrate their emotional experiences. It contrasts with dissociation by encouraging active engagement with emotional discomfort rather than avoidance. Grounding can be supported by various activities, such as moving the body, eating healthily, and engaging in creative arts, all of which contribute to a more grounded and focused state of being.

Defining Your Boundaries: As discussed in *The Language of Emotions* by McLaren (2010), it focuses on establishing and reinforcing personal boundaries, which are essential for mental and emotional well-being. This practice involves a visualization technique where one imagines a bubble encircling oneself, symbolizing their personal space. This mental image acts as a tool to create and strengthen a sense of privacy and separation, enabling individuals to acknowledge and assert their rightful personal space, often overlooked in daily life.

Personal boundaries are perceived physically and emotionally, noticeable in situations like being uncomfortable under someone's gaze or in a crowded environment. In the modern world, where distractions are common, many struggle to recognize and maintain their boundaries, leading to a disconnection from their inner selves. This practice addresses this by grounding oneself and focusing inward, fostering a more defined sense of self and stronger personal boundaries.

The exercise also highlights the role of emotions in setting and maintaining boundaries. Emotions such as anger and shame are crucial for identifying and responding to boundary violations, whether from external sources or oneself. Similarly, fear and sadness are important in upholding these boundaries and personal space. Understanding and effectively managing these emotions is key to developing a healthy sense of self and boundaries.

Regular practice of this visualization, alongside grounding and focusing exercises, is recommended to strengthen one's sense of personal space and boundaries. This ongoing practice benefits individual mental and emotional health and positively impacts emotional intelligence, self-awareness, and interpersonal interactions.

Burning Contracts: Burning contracts are an integral part of the emotional channeling process described in *The Language of Emotions* by McLaren (2010). This technique begins by grounding within personal boundaries, creating a space for emotional processing. Participants are guided to visualize a metaphorical parchment within this space, upon which they can project various distress-related elements. These elements include emotional expectations, intellectual stances, physical rules, spiritual expectations, and specific situations or relationships that cause distress.

Different emotions may arise as these elements are mentally placed onto the parchment. The exercise encourages welcoming these emotions, using them to understand and gain control over the distressing aspects. Emotions like anger, fear, grief, or depression are acknowledged and channeled according to the needs of the moment.

Once the parchment is filled with these elements, symbolizing the emotional contracts, it is rolled up tightly. This action represents the commitment to these distressing thoughts and behaviors. The next step involves symbolically disposing of this contract by imagining throwing it outside the personal boundary and burning it with appropriate emotional energy. This act symbolizes the release and liberation from these unhelpful elements.

The practice concludes with reflecting on changes in one's emotional state, personal boundaries, or surrounding environment. Such changes indicate progress in the emotional channeling process. "Burning Contracts" is a powerful tool for releasing negative emotions and patterns, leading to personal understanding and transformation. This practice can be flexibly incorporated into daily life, allowing individuals to actively work towards emotional well-being and liberation from unfulfilling behaviors and attitudes.

Conscious Complaining: A structured approach for intentionally expressing frustrations in a controlled environment. This practice begins with the individual selecting a private space where they can openly and freely express their grievances, absurdities, or challenges. The key aspect of this exercise is to acknowledge the intention to complain, using a phrase like "I'm complaining now!" to mark the beginning of the process.

During the exercise, individuals are encouraged to fully articulate their negative emotions and thoughts. This expression can incorporate sarcasm or humor to facilitate the release of pent-up emotions, making the process more effective and less burdensome. The goal is to allow a safe and unrestricted outlet for feelings that are typically repressed, which helps in alleviating mental stagnation and enhancing emotional flow.

Upon concluding the expression of complaints, the exercise involves a gesture of gratitude directed towards the chosen recipient of the complaint, whether it be an inanimate object or a natural element. This step is crucial as it helps transition from releasing negative emotions to a more positive state. The practice then concludes with engaging in a pleasurable activity, further balancing complaining with an uplifting experience.

McLaren (2010) emphasizes that "Conscious Complaining" is particularly effective in breaking through emotional and mental blockages, significantly contributing to restoring a sense of well-being. This practice is a valuable tool for managing emotions, especially when feeling overwhelmed or mentally cluttered, and can be easily incorporated into one's routine as needed.

Rejuvenation: The "Rejuvenation" exercise, as described by McLaren (2010), is designed to refresh and restore emotional well-being, particularly following periods of intense emotional experiences or significant life changes. The exercise commences with the individual finding a comfortable position and engaging in gentle breathing, establishing a grounding connection to the present. This foundational step prepares the individual for the restorative process.

Next, the individual is encouraged to engage constructively with the emotion of fear to sharpen their present-moment focus and visualize a personal boundary, representing a safe and contained space for emotional processing.

Within this space, the individual imagines a favorite place, employing all senses in the visualization to foster a sense of peace and beauty. This immersive experience is meant to infuse the individual with tranquility and contentment.

The final stage involves allowing the body and mind to relax completely, enhancing this state by physically touching the floor and letting the head hang, symbolizing tension release and deeper grounding. McLaren (2010) highlights the importance of this practice in contemporary life, where it's easy to be caught up in distractions and overlook the need for self-care. The "Rejuvenation" exercise is a versatile tool for maintaining emotional equilibrium. It can be easily integrated into daily routines to help balance the demands of emotional work with life's simpler joys.

Consciously Question Your Emotions or Feelings

1. Begin with a Clear Opening Statement

Initiate your Conscious Questioning session with a statement like, "Now, I'm going to consciously explore what I'm feeling."

2. Questioning the Emotion or Feeling

Direct your attention to the emotion or feeling you are experiencing and start a dialogue with it.

Here are some guided questions to help you delve deeper:

Identifying the Emotion or Feeling:

What is the primary emotion I'm feeling right now?

Can I label it simply (e.g., happiness, sadness, anger, fear, disgust)?

Understanding Its Roots:

What triggered this emotion or feeling?

Have I felt this way in similar situations in the past?

Recognizing Physical Sensations:

Where in my body do I feel this emotion or feeling?

What physical sensations are associated with it (e.g., tightness, warmth, restlessness)?

Exploring the Emotion or Feeling's Purpose:

What might this emotion be trying to tell or teach me?

Is this emotion or feeling a reaction to a current event, or is it reflecting something deeper from my past experiences?

Assessing the Impact:

How does this emotion of feeling affect my thoughts and behaviors?

Is this feeling influencing my decision-making or relationships?

Seeking Constructive Outcomes:

What can I do right now to address or embrace this emotion or feeling?

Are there any positive actions I can take to channel this emotion constructively?

Reflection and Perspective:

How would I advise a friend who was feeling this way?

Can I view this situation from a different perspective?

3. Conclude with a Closing Statement

When you feel your session is complete, end with a statement like, "I acknowledge and understand what I am feeling. I love, accept, and value what my emotions are telling me. Now, I'm concluding my exploration."

By learning to identify, understand, and accept our emotional experiences, we empower ourselves to navigate life's complexities with greater awareness and compassion. Embracing our emotions as valuable messengers, we cultivate a deeper connection with our inner selves and enhance our overall emotional well-being. Remember, every emotion is a part of our journey, offering insights and opportunities for growth. As we close this chapter, let us carry forward the wisdom gained from our explorations, cherishing the profound impact of self-reflection and emotional literacy in our lives.

CHAPTER 3

The Day We All Changed Forever

"There is no pain so great as the memory of joy in present grief." —Aeschylus

It was the day our lives took an irreversible turn, a day etched into the fabric of our existence. The ripple effects of our profound loss alter the course of our lives forever. In the quiet early hours, our world shifted. Before that fateful day, our life was a tapestry of solid relationships, defined roles, and unwavering faith.

That day, we all changed forever. It's a universal truth that life is fraught with moments of unbearable sorrow, and this chapter begins our navigating through the aftermath of one such moment.

Her Quest for Enlightened Comprehension:

On the day my son Trevor passed away, a part of me felt like it shattered, too. Everything changed when Trevor's heart unexpectedly stopped in the early morning hours.

An overwhelming sense of panic and trauma surrounded me as a medical team worked tirelessly for 90 minutes to revive him. In that room filled with prayers, I clung to the hope that the blip on the monitor would signify a miracle. As I walked into the emergency room, I held onto the belief of miracles, anticipating that God would grant the miracle needed for us to return to our everyday, normal family life.

But the expected miracle didn't unfold. The medical team, their eyes filled with empathy, took turns administering compressions on Trevor's chest, pausing to watch the monitor for a sign that never materialized. The trauma of that moment is etched into my body, heart, and soul. The team respectfully inquired about stopping, and Trevor, who just yesterday was perfect, lay there; the only trauma now evident was from the CPR that unfortunately didn't work.

With tears in our eyes, my husband and I nodded to halt the efforts. The medical team shifted their focus, delicately cleaning Trevor up and removing the equipment that, moments ago, held the promise of a miracle. A nurse gently wrapped Trevor in a sheet and placed him in my arms. My healthy 6-year-old, who played in the backyard just the day before, was now gone.

There was no visible trauma on Trevor, leaving me to grapple with the incomprehensible reality of his heart just stopping. Like a profound crack in the universe, everything about me – my life, physical being, and well-being – crumbled. The anticipated miracle never arrived, and I was left to navigate through the fragments of an altered reality.

His Path of Insightful Realization:

Our world irreversibly shifted that day. We became a family reduced by one. I recall the sheriff deputy's presence, his questions forming a surreal backdrop to our unfolding nightmare. Neighbors gathered, their faces etched with tears and disbelief, mirroring our shock and despair.

The details of that day are etched in my mind: the medical staff's faces, a canvas of exhaustion and empathy as they worked tirelessly to revive Trevor. Their eyes eventually sought ours, a silent plea for permission to cease the futile battle against the inevitable.

A haunting quiet settled over our home in the wake of Trevor's departure. His absence was a tangible void. His brothers no longer had him to play with, his laughter and mischief forever silenced. Trevor's bedroom stood empty, a stark, unoccupied space where dreams and stories once lived.

Our social landscape transformed overnight. Friends, unsure how to navigate the chasm of our loss, began to drift away, leaving a sense of abandonment in their wake. The world continued its pace around us, yet we were anchored in that moment of loss, unable to move forward. That day, the day Trevor died, marked not just the loss of a beloved son and brother but the shattering of our normalcy. Our family's journey through grief began in those harrowing moments, a journey of navigating a world forever altered.

About Trevor

Our precious son, Trevor, passed of SUDC (Sudden Unexplained Death in Childhood) in August 2014 at six and a half years old. Those who knew Trevor remember him as a very energetic, kind child. Trevor was known by many names: T-man, Mr. T, Tornado Trev. He loved wearing mismatched socks, playing with friends, making new friends, and jamming his guitar. He was a volunteer in his community (always with a smile) and understood the concept of giving back at an early age.

Trevor cherished his role as both a younger and older brother. He was so excited to be a big brother finally! He was always so caring toward his younger brother. Trevor and his older brother, who was only 16 months his senior, did everything together: sleepovers, soccer lessons, and creating with Legos. Their shared adventures were full of joy and companionship. Trevor's interactions with his older sister were filled with laughter and fun.

Trevor's emotional intelligence was remarkable for his age; he always knew how to comfort and uplift those around him, never hesitating to step in and be just what they needed. Even when Mom or Dad cooked the most mundane thing for dinner, he would always get off his chair, hug us, and say, "This dinner is amazing." He always tried new foods but would comment, "That is interesting but not my favorite," if he disliked something.

He had such determination in life! We remember tucking him into bed after a tough day of learning to ride his 2-wheel bike. He said, "Tomorrow, I WILL get it." The next day, he woke up and went right outside to his bike. It wasn't long after that determination that he was successfully riding his bike! He was SO proud, and we were proud of him, too.

His sudden and confusing departure from this life has altered us in ways we are still learning. We miss the level of activity that the three boys brought to the house or watching their bond grow. We miss the happiness that we all embraced when he was here. We have tried so hard to put one foot in front of the other because Trevor would not want us to be sad, but he is hard to live without. He is missed by his family and friends so very much.

While we miss the energy and happiness he brought into our lives, we strive to move forward, honoring his wish for us not to dwell in sadness but rather help those in grief because that is what he would do.

CHAPTER 4

A Stranger in My Own Life: Navigating Loss and Rebuilding Identity

"I am not what happened to me, I am what I choose to become." —Carl Jung

As we opened the door to our home, a place that had once been a sanctuary of familiarity, an overwhelming sense of unfamiliarity washed over us. The walls echoed with the haunting absence of laughter, and the rooms seemed to have rearranged themselves in a silent rebellion against the known. It was as if the essence of our being had been displaced, and we stood in the doorway, strangers in our own life.

In those initial moments, the disconnection was palpable. Every step felt like a tentative exploration of foreign territory, and the air held a weight of unspoken grief. The home that had once embraced the rhythms of family life now stood as a testament to the void left by the absence of a beloved son.

The journey through grief often feels like navigating uncharted territory, with emotions shifting like unpredictable tides. We stand before the mirror, gazing at the reflection that once felt so familiar. But today, the eyes staring back seem like those of strangers. If this is your reality, if grief has made you a stranger in your own life, know that you're not alone. In this chapter, we explore the complexities of this emotional journey, seeking connection amid the void.

Her Quest for Enlightened Comprehension:

Who I was versus who I am now – two distinct entities separated by the profound gulf of loss. The lens through which I view the world has shifted, and every moment is inevitably categorized as either before or after Trevor passed away. It's not a conscious choice; it just is. Reflecting on my past, I don't see myself; instead, there's a hazy figure bearing a resemblance to me, yet unfamiliar. Those memories are elusive, slipping through my fingers like grains of sand.

Yet, each day demanded a fresh start – energy depleted, answers absent, children in need of parents, and a society expecting resilience. The perception of the person I used to be lingered, a ghost haunting the determined, type-A personality who seemingly had all the answers. Little did they know that within me resided a stranger grappling with the unimaginable. Tasks I used to be good at were suddenly beyond my ability.

I found myself reacting to things that never bothered me before. For example, a family visited us at our home after Trevor passed. Their child wore a zip-up sweatshirt covering their face; on it was a skeleton. Seemingly innocent, it was certainly the trend at that time. But this skeleton set off a reaction of upset, panic, and anger within me. Suddenly, the image of a skeleton, once a harmless fashion statement, became a stark reminder of my loss, evoking a visceral response that was both unexpected and overwhelming. This experience taught me a crucial lesson about grief; it is a complex and often unpredictable journey. Each person's triggers are unique and can lead to a flood of emotions, even from the most mundane sources. To this day, nine years later, skeletons are not a pleasant thing for me to see, but I have come a long way in learning how to manage my reactions during those moments that could incite panic. We will talk about this in the chapter on the nervous system.

I began to understand that these reactions were emotional and physical. My heart raced, my palms sweated, and I felt a tightness in my chest – classic signs of panic. It was a testament to how deeply our bodies and minds are interconnected, especially during intense emotional stress.

As a grief coach, I now recognize that this experience has highlighted the importance of being gentle with ourselves when faced with unexpected triggers. It's crucial to acknowledge and validate these feelings rather than dismissing or judging them. In this book, my aim is to provide strategies for coping with such moments, stressing the importance of self-compassion and empathetic insight as we navigate the unpredictable journey of grief.

His Path of Insightful Realization:

The most profound transformation occurred in how I perceived the world around me. The once-comforting sight of my family sleeping peacefully evoked a sense of dread. Each still form now resembled a lifeless body, compelling me to check for signs of life – a gentle breath or a subtle movement. I performed this ritual night after night, seeking assurance in their breathing. It was as though death, having once entered our lives so unexpectedly, now cast a persistent, ominous shadow over the simplest, most mundane moments, constantly reminding me of life's inherent fragility.

Sleep, which used to be a refuge, transformed into a battleground of the mind. Instead of rest, I found myself deep in thought. My thoughts were entangled in an unyielding cycle, relentlessly revisiting memories of Trevor's life and the stark reality of his death. This relentless mental playback drained me at night and continued into the day. Even the simplest tasks took on monumental proportions, their simplicity belied by the weight of grief. The routine and mundane became laborious, each action a reminder of the profound change that had enveloped my life. My brain, once a reliable tool for tackling life's challenges, now seemed trapped in an endless state of mourning. Mental resources necessary for clarity and decision-making were missing in action, and self-doubt began to infiltrate my identity, especially in my role as a parent. A sea of questions and uncertainties now replaced the confidence with which I had once navigated parenthood. Could I continue to parent effectively while being swept up in this maelstrom of grief? Each decision and action felt like navigating through a fog without a compass, the innate parental instincts that once guided me were now shrouded in haze.

Research Perspectives:

Grief is a journey through uncharted emotional territories, and when the familiar landscape of our lives is altered by loss, we find ourselves becoming strangers in our existence. Feeling like a stranger in one's life can be a disorienting and transformative experience. This chapter delves into the Research Perspectives of experts in the field of grief, offering insights to help readers navigate this complex terrain. Drawing on the work of Therese Rando, George Bonanno, and Bessel van der Kolk, we explore the psychological and somatic dimensions of feeling like a stranger in the grieving process.

Comprehending the Rhythms of Grief

Therese Rando, a pioneering grief psychologist, introduced the "Six R's of Mourning" framework to understand the multifaceted grieving process. The first step, Recognizing, involves acknowledging the permanence of the absence, a fundamental shift in one's reality. This recognition paves the way for the subsequent task of Reacting to the following emotional upheaval. As grief unfolds, Remembering with love becomes a poignant task, transforming mourning into a tribute to the departed. The journey then leads to tasks of Reconstructing life without the loved one, Reconciling the emotional turbulence, and ultimately, Relinquishing old attachments, allowing for a gradual acceptance of the new normal (Rando, 1986).

William Worden, a leading figure in grief counseling, proposed a model encapsulated in the "Tasks of Mourning." The initial task involves accepting the reality of the loss and acknowledging the profound shift in one's world. Following acceptance, the grieving individual is faced with the task of processing the pain associated with the departure. Subsequently, the journey encompasses adjusting to a life without the physical presence of the loved one – a gradual process demanding patience and self-compassion. The final task involves finding a way to maintain a connection while adapting to the new normal, striking a delicate balance between honoring the memory and embracing the present (Worden, 2009).

Embodied Grief:

Bessel van der Kolk, a leading expert on trauma and the body, provides a lens through which to examine the embodied aspect of feeling like a stranger. In *The Body Keeps the Score: Brain, Mind, and Body in the Healing of Trauma*, van der Kolk explores how trauma, including grief, can become stored in the body. The physical sensations of disconnection experienced when feeling like a stranger may be manifestations of this embodied grief. Integrating somatic approaches, such as mindfulness and body-centered therapies, can be instrumental in reconnecting with the self and easing the tension that accompanies this disorientation (van der Kolk, 2014).

Navigating Loss: Suggestions & Support

Here, you will find practical strategies and thoughtful advice to support you in rediscovering who you are and who you might become after your world has been irrevocably changed. This journey is about coping with the absence of a loved one and embracing the transformation within yourself, finding your footing in a life that may now feel unfamiliar.

Relearning Self: An Actionable Task for Navigating Grief

The struggle persisted for years before the full weight of the impact became clear. I faced a choice: resist this new reality with all my might or surrender to it, allowing the scattered pieces of my life to fall into place organically, not dictated by my insistence but guided by the slow process of acceptance.

Grief is an intricate dance with one's own identity. Here is an actionable task to guide individuals through relearning who they are amidst the challenging landscape of loss. This task is inspired by Therese Rando's "Six R's of Mourning" and William Worden's "Tasks of Mourning."

Recognize Your Changed Reality: Acknowledge the profound shift in your world. Understand that the loss has altered your identity, and it's okay to feel disoriented.

React to the Emotional Waves: Embrace the emotional upheaval that accompanies grief. Allow yourself to feel without judgment. Journaling can be a helpful tool to express and process these emotions.

Remember with Love: Engage in a heartfelt exploration of memories. Create a space for remembrance, whether through a memorial, a scrapbook, or simply revisiting shared experiences in your mind.

Reconcile with the New Normal: Practice self-compassion as you navigate the challenges of your new reality. Understand that the journey of grief is not linear; it involves periods of adjustment and readjustment.

Craft a New Narrative: Embrace the opportunity to craft a new narrative for your life that acknowledges the impact of loss and allows for growth, resilience, and the emergence of a redefined identity.

Remember, this task is a gradual and personalized journey. It's about reclaiming agency over your narrative, allowing for the coexistence of grief and the rediscovery of self.

It's important to remember that rebuilding your identity in the aftermath of loss is a deeply personal and ongoing process. The suggestions and support offered here are stepping stones to healing and self-discovery. Grief can challenge the very essence of our being, yet it also has the potential to unveil new insights about ourselves and our role in the world. As you continue your journey, be gentle with yourself and embrace the changes with courage and hope. The path to rediscovering your identity may be winding and uncertain. Still, it is also a path filled with potential for growth, resilience, and a deeper appreciation for the intricacies of life. Carry these insights and strategies with you as you navigate the complexities of loss and rebuild a sense of self that your experiences have changed and enriched.

CHAPTER 5

Navigating the Haze:
The First Few Months

"Grief is like a fog; it sits heavily on your heart and obscures everything else." —Unknown

In the first few months following Trevor's passing, our world transformed into an unfamiliar landscape, deeply shadowed by grief. It felt like we had descended into an abyss, a realm where even the most familiar aspects of life seemed distorted and strange. Each day unfolded within a thick haze, clouding our vision and turning the routine tasks of life into monumental challenges.

We remember waking up each morning to a surreal and painfully sharp reality. Simple activities, like making a cup of coffee or driving to the grocery store, became Herculean feats, requiring an effort that seemed to drain the very essence of our beings. The world around us continued in its usual rhythm, yet we felt disconnected, as if watching life through a foggy lens. The vibrant colors that once painted our lives together with Trevor now appeared dull and muted. Conversations turned into a series of distant echoes, and laughter from others seemed like a foreign language. We found ourselves moving through the days on autopilot, performing tasks mechanically, devoid of the joy and engagement that once accompanied them.

In this haze, the passage of time became elusive. Hours stretched into days, and days melded into one another, each marked by the relentless weight of absence. The nights were particularly challenging, as the quiet allowed our thoughts to echo louder, reminding us of the gaping void left by Trevor's absence.

Yet, during this disorienting fog, there were moments of clarity – brief instances where memories of Trevor brought both pain and a strange comfort. In these fleeting moments, we felt a connection to the love we shared, a reminder that even in the deepest sorrow, there remained a glimmer of the life we had built together.

This chapter delves into the heart of those first few months, exploring the complexities of navigating a world that has shifted on its axis. It is a candid reflection on our struggles dealing with the mundane when our hearts were entrenched in mourning. It aims to provide a voice to those silent battles fought in the wake of loss and, in doing so, perhaps offer a sense of solidarity and empathy to others walking through their haze of grief.

Her Quest for Enlightened Comprehension:

In those initial months, every waking moment was a struggle. The simple act of getting out of bed felt like lifting a mountain. I moved through life as if encased in a fog, the clarity of purpose lost in the jumble of emotions. Muscle memory took over, propelling me through the motions of daily survival.

Navigating any public space became a surreal experience. The "real" world is so incredibly harsh to someone in grief. Loud noise, any sense of rudeness, or stress feels like it could send me into a pile of tears at any given moment. I used to joke that I wished I could have "please handle with care" across my forehead. Maybe people would notice and be kinder? Or excuse my absent-minded step into their path or my long gaze as I forgot why I was there or what I was supposed to do next. Even the once mundane task of grocery shopping now felt like an expedition into an alien world. I'd catch myself reaching for items Trevor loved, only to remember he was no longer here to enjoy them, and I'd think, what is the quickest way out of this store because I do not have the strength to get what we need? The unconscious expectation of his presence lingered like a ghost, a constant reminder of the void he had left behind.

Even the most minor details triggered overwhelming grief – a familiar scent, a forgotten toy, or an empty chair at the dinner table. I was raised with a robust work ethic and a sense of responsibility. My life, for the most part, had been relatively calm and blessed, but I had encountered adversity in various forms – an injury, challenges at work, and familial discord. Who I was then believed one must tough it out in tough times – muscle through, exert more effort, and push forward. Retreat was never an option in my worldview.

When Trevor passed away, this belief system took center stage in my mind. I had an action plan. My family depended on me to remain functional and provide for them. The surviving kids needed grief support; they had just lost their best friend. My goal was simple: to function and support our kids. My determination was unwavering. Two weeks after Trevor's passing, I returned to work. I was experiencing panic attacks, grief bursts, chest pain, headaches, anxiety, and the constant annoyance of eye twitching. Yet, I was working. Initially, I was grateful for the distraction. There were brief moments when I immersed myself in a work task, and for a minute or two, the enormity of the loss wasn't the first thing on my mind. However, I realized, and this remains true years later, that the loss would always run as a loop in my mind. Imagine 15 windows open on a computer screen – one of those windows is my Trevor window, a perpetual connection to my child who is no longer physically present but alive in my memories.

To those outside my immediate family, it seemed like function and perseverance. People didn't see or inquire that we were crawling through each day. My husband and I had every ounce of energy dedicated to getting through the day. Dinners were often just cereal or whatever we could grab and eat, if I ate at all. School events for the kids, unless mandatory, were not a priority. Life events outside of showing up to work were not either. We could get our son to his extracurricular event and then home. Weekends were spent trying to recharge our empty reserves to face the upcoming week.

We had our oldest son in therapy, which we deemed crucial. We still parent the youngest, but not like before. We weren't those people anymore. "Muscle through" became "be a robot." Robot mode served me well; I was functioning. To others, we appeared to be intact and operational. Deadlines were met, responsibilities were primarily accomplished, and life continued. I repeated the same actions five days a week, only to collapse in exhaustion on the weekends, where I would sit as much as possible. I didn't want to do anything. This cycle repeated month after month. While I occasionally sought things to help myself, I never prioritized it. While "angry robot mode" served as a necessary function to keep life moving, I've come to understand there's a more healing-oriented approach. Moving away from the suppression characteristic of "robot mode," embracing the acknowledgment and processing of emotions paves the way for healthier coping mechanisms.

Practices like journaling and mindfulness aid in building emotional resilience and emphasize the crucial role of self-care and compassion. During these challenging times, being kind to oneself isn't just beneficial; it's essential. Grief coaching plays a pivotal role here, setting realistic and personal goals for the healing journey. It recognizes that each individual's path to healing is distinct. Moreover, it underscores the importance of social support and connection, providing a lifeline from the isolation that often accompanies grief. Ultimately, this approach guides individuals in weaving their loss into the fabric of their lives meaningfully, allowing space to honor their loved ones while fostering personal growth and new perspectives.

His Path of Insightful Realization:

In the days and weeks following Trevor's passing, my life settled into a routine that felt both necessary and numbing. Tasks were mechanical and devoid of the vibrant energy that once defined me and our home. Each day became a sequence of motions to be performed, a way to keep moving forward when every part of me wanted to stand still in my grief. Mornings began with the mechanical process of getting ready for work, a task that seemed trivial in the grand scheme of things yet provided a semblance of normalcy for our surviving kids. The muscle memory of parenting took over, but a hollow ache replaced the joy.

Nightfall brought its own rituals. The glow of the television offered little comfort, merely serving as background noise to my thoughts. Then, I would pour myself a drink, a glass of whiskey that seemed to momentarily dull reality's sharp edges. One new ritual was my nightly conversations with Trevor and God. Even as winter approached, I found myself under the vast expanse of the night sky, speaking to Trevor, seeking his presence in the whisper of the wind and the stars that blinked overhead. These one-sided conversations were my way of keeping him close, of trying to bridge the gap between life and loss. In those quiet moments, I was reaching out for something greater, a plea for guidance, insight, and comfort from a higher power. The conversations with God were filled with questions and pleas for solace, a search for meaning in the incomprehensible tapestry of life and death. This routine, this daily journey through grief and ritual, became my lifeline in the haze of those first few months. It was a path marked by sorrow, longing, and the unending quest for peace in a world irrevocably altered by loss.

Research Perspectives:

Grief is an intricate journey, and the first few months often unfold as a complex dance between shock, routine, and the search for meaning. Drawing from the insights of experts in the field, we aim to shed light on the psychological underpinnings of navigating this initial haze of grief. Drawing upon a wealth of studies and expert insights, we aim to shed light on the common experiences and challenges faced during this initial period of mourning. This section is intended to provide a framework for comprehending the intense emotions, cognitive changes, and physical reactions often accompanying the early months of grief. Our goal is to offer validation for these experiences and insights into how they are reflected in broader scientific research, providing a bridge between personal experience and professional comprehension.

Understanding the Mechanisms of Grief

Therese Rando emphasizes that individuals often enter a state of shock or disbelief in the initial stages. The autopilot survival mode, as we experienced it, aligns with Bonanno's concept of resilience.

Therese Rando, a clinical psychologist known for her work on grief and mourning, provides a comprehensive framework for comprehending the adaptive nature of mourning and the mechanisms at play during the early stages of grief. Rando's model emphasizes the adaptive nature of mourning, suggesting that individuals often enter a state of shock or disbelief when faced with profound loss. This shock can manifest as a form of autopilot survival, a way for the mind to protect itself from the overwhelming reality of the situation (Rando, 1993).

In our experience, the autopilot survival mode meant going through the motions of daily life without fully grasping the emotional weight of our loss. Tasks once infused with purpose became mechanical routines, and the world felt like a blurry landscape devoid of color. Rando's model allows us to contextualize this autopilot response as a natural phase in the grieving process – one that provides a temporary shield against the full impact of the loss.

Resilience in the Face of Adversity

George Bonanno's (2009) research on resilience adds another layer to our comprehension of navigating the haze of grief. Bonanno defines resilience as the ability to maintain psychological and emotional well-being in the face of adversity. The autopilot survival mode can be seen as a manifestation of this resilience. This coping mechanism allows individuals to carry on with daily life while grappling with the profound changes brought about by loss.

Bonanno's work challenges the notion that there is a universal "right" way to grieve. Instead, he highlights the diversity of responses to loss, with resilience being a common thread among those who navigate grief uniquely. This empowering insight reminds us that there is no one-size-fits-all approach to mourning. As a form of resilience, the autopilot survival mode becomes a valid and adaptive response to the challenges of the early grieving period – the ability to maintain psychological and emotional well-being in the face of adversity (Bonanno, 2009).

In concluding this research section, we reflect on the profound insights from exploring the academic and clinical perspectives on early-stage grief. The studies and expert opinions we've discussed here provide a valuable context for comprehending the maze of emotions and challenges we faced in the first few months after losing Trevor. This body of research underscores the complexity of grief and validates the myriad ways it manifests in those initial, disorienting months.

In hindsight, it becomes clear that this phase of grief, though incredibly challenging, serves a vital purpose in both your immediate survival and future healing. It acts as a crucial buffer, allowing you to gradually process the initial shock and intense emotions at a pace your mind and body can withstand. While often painful and disorienting, this adjustment period lays the groundwork for the longer journey of healing that follows. It's a testament to the human capacity to endure and eventually adapt to life-changing events, providing a foundation for future growth and insight.

We hope that by sharing these research findings, we can offer comfort and guidance to others who find themselves in the haze of early grief, helping to illuminate a path through the confusion and reaffirming that they are not alone in their journey. This section is a testament to the resilience of the human spirit in the face of profound loss and a reminder that, even in our darkest hours, there is knowledge and understanding to light the way.

Navigating Loss: Suggestions & Support

As we reflect on the early stages of our journey through grief, it becomes evident that every phase, particularly the initial one, plays a significant role in the overall process of healing. This section is dedicated to exploring and shedding light on the crucial role that the early phase of grief plays in both our survival and eventual healing. In hindsight, we recognize that this period, characterized by intense emotions and disorientation, is not just a phase to endure but a critical step in adapting to a life-altering loss. As a grief coach and someone who has traversed the challenging terrain of loss, my goal is to bridge the gap between the wisdom offered by experts and the realities of personal experience.

In providing actionable guidance, my intention is to assist those grappling with the intricate complexities of grief. Firstly, it's crucial to recognize the autopilot mechanisms at play within your unique journey. Navigating the haze is a natural response to profound loss, and it's entirely acceptable if the world around you appears mechanical and routine during this phase. Embrace the realization that the autopilot survival mode is an innate response deeply rooted in resilience. This realization grants you the freedom to traverse this phase without self-judgment. It acknowledges that it's a significant step in the grieving process and sets the foundation for future healing and growth.

To facilitate this journey, consider the following practical steps, drawing inspiration from the insights of experts like Rando and Bonanno:

Acknowledge the Autopilot: Recognize and accept the autopilot response as a natural coping mechanism in the face of grief. Comprehending its presence allows you to navigate its impact more consciously.

Understand the Natural Response: Comprehend that the haze you may be experiencing is a natural and adaptive reaction to loss. This acknowledgment can help ease the burden of self-expectations during this challenging period.

Embrace the Mechanical and Routine: It's okay if your surroundings seem mechanical and routine. This phase is part of the grieving process; allowing yourself to move through it without judgment is key to healing.

Seek Moments of Connection: Even amid the shadows of grief, actively seek moments of connection with yourself and others. Share memories, express your emotions, and find solace in the shared experience of navigating loss.

Navigate Together: Grieving is unfamiliar, but you don't have to navigate it alone. Together, we can find glimpses of hope amidst the autopilot survival. By acknowledging the natural responses and integrating these practical steps, you empower yourself to move through the haze with resilience and self-compassion.

In concluding this section, we recognize that the initial phase of grief, with all its pain and confusion, is a pivotal part of the healing journey. It serves as a necessary period of adjustment, where the mind and body learn to cope with the new reality of loss. Though often overwhelming, this phase is a testament to our resilience and capacity for healing. It lays the groundwork for the long, transformative process of recovery, helping us gradually rebuild and find meaning again. As we look back, we understand that this early stage of grief is not just about survival; it is about beginning the path toward healing, a journey that reshapes our comprehension of loss, love, and life itself.

CHAPTER 6

Healing the Nervous System: A Symphony of Self-Care

"Grief is more than an emotion; it is a wave that engulfs the whole body and being." —Unknown

At the time of Trevor's passing, we had very little experience with mental health. Our knowledge was limited, perhaps shadowed by societal stigmas and a lack of personal exposure to the intricate workings of the human psyche. Trevor's loss thrust us into a realm where mental and emotional well-being became not just relevant but crucial to our survival. We would later become aware of the nervous system and the impact that we were contending with. This realization dawned gradually as we started to understand that the profound changes we were experiencing went far beyond emotional turmoil; they were deeply rooted in the very biology of our being. The nervous system, an intricate network that had seamlessly orchestrated our responses to the world, was now in disarray, mirroring the chaos of our shattered hearts.

In this state of heightened sensitivity, our bodies respond to grief with a primal urgency. We noticed how our physical reactions were intertwined with our emotional states. The tightening of the chest, the quickening of the pulse, the unsettling restlessness – these were not just metaphors of grief but tangible manifestations of a nervous system under siege. It was as if our bodies were sounding alarms, reacting to the loss of Trevor as a visceral threat to our existence.

As we delved deeper into comprehending the nervous system's role in grief, we began to see the importance of addressing our physical as well as emotional health. We learned that stress hormones like cortisol and adrenaline were coursing through our bodies, keeping us in a constant state of alert, disrupting sleep, and impacting our overall health. The nervous system, in its attempt to cope with the trauma, was inadvertently amplifying our suffering.

This insight was a turning point in our journey. For one, it allowed for some realization that our current "status" was somewhat out of our control, or was it? We realized that healing had to be holistic, encompassing mind, body, and spirit. We explored various practices to soothe and reset our nervous system. Techniques like mindfulness meditation, deep breathing exercises, and gentle yoga became tools for mental relaxation and physiological recalibration. We discovered the healing power of nature and how a few simple minutes in the sunshine could bring a semblance of peace to our frayed nerves.

In sharing this part of our story, we aim to highlight the often-overlooked physical dimension of grief. Distinguishing the nervous system's response to loss is crucial in healing. It's a journey of integrating self-care practices that honor the mind and the body, recognizing that they are inseparably connected in the tapestry of our grief and healing. We hope that by shedding light on this aspect, we can help others navigate their path through loss with greater awareness and compassion for their whole selves.

The nervous system, a symphony of responses, orchestrates our reactions to the world around us. Yet, in the wake of profound loss, this symphony can be disrupted, leading to a cacophony of emotions and physical responses. In this chapter, we explore the profound impact of grief on the nervous system and present strategies for a healing journey.

Her Quest for Enlightened Comprehension:

In the wake of Trevor's passing, every fiber of my being felt frayed, and the impact on my nervous system was profound, like nothing I had ever experienced. I had always had "stress" in my life, but this was more like an oppression over every aspect of my being. Simple tasks, like answering the phone or opening the mail, triggered a cascade of anxiety. Sleep became elusive, as I seemed stuck in a perpetual alert state. The echoes of loss haunted the quiet of the night, checking on my husband or our kids to see if they were still breathing. Trying to approach how I felt was too scary even to begin. I felt that once I began, I would never stop. So, I forced most of what I felt to stay away by staying in motion and busy. My eye twitched nonstop. It is somewhat humorous but mostly annoying. A subtle sign that all was not well with my nervous system. Then, the panic attacks started. Sometimes, I couldn't even tell what triggered them. I had a persistent tightness in my chest, trying to catch my breath, shaking, and a headache that lingered for hours. Like uninvited guests, a general sense of restlessness became a daily companion as I knew anything could set the next one off. The nervous system, once a reliable ally in maintaining equilibrium, now felt like a traitor, hijacked by the grief that had taken residence in my soul.

His Path of Insightful Realization:

In the months following Trevor's passing, a subtle yet significant change had taken root in my very being. Unbeknownst to me, I found myself caught in a pattern of shallow breathing, a physical manifestation of my mind's relentless replay of that fateful morning. It was as if my body was unconsciously mirroring the constriction of my heart, each shallow breath a reflection of the pain that gripped me. This involuntary response became more noticeable as I found myself repeatedly reliving the details of Trevor's death and the stomach upset that came with the shallow breathing. My mind would painstakingly dissect every moment, playing the events forward and backward. It felt like I was trapped in that specific time frame, unable to move forward yet incapable of going back. The world around me continued its relentless march, but I remained anchored in that moment, trapped in a loop of grief and memory.

The intensity of this memory, with its vivid imagery and raw emotion, often left me feeling physically and emotionally drained. It was a silent struggle, a private torment that echoed the depth of my loss and seemed unrelenting, a constant companion in my journey through grief. It would take us years, but we eventually found out about memory reprocessing, a way to process the trauma of that morning. Although long overdue, we were finally attending to our grief, and the vice-like grip of those memories began to loosen. I could finally view the events of that morning from a distance, to acknowledge the pain without being consumed by it. It was as if a window had been opened in a long-sealed room, letting in light and air, offering a fresh perspective on a memory that had once seemed suffocating. As I combined self-care with healing and insight, I also noticed subtle shifts in my physical responses. The shallow breathing that had become a reflex began to give way to deeper, more intentional breaths, signaling a newfound control over my body's response to grief.

Research Perspectives:

Grief, a profound emotional response to loss, intricately weaves its threads into the fabric of our nervous system, affecting the very core of our being (Porges, 2011). In this section, we explore the research from leading experts in trauma, grief psychology, somatic therapy, and memory consolidation to illuminate the intricate dance between grief and the nervous system. Drawing on their insights, we aim to provide actionable guidance for those seeking holistic self-care and healing.

Comprehending the Nervous System in Grief:
A Framework for Healing

In the aftermath of loss, the nervous system often undergoes significant challenges, manifesting in a range of physical and emotional responses. To navigate this complex terrain, we turn to the expert insights of Steven Porges and Peter Levine and key insights from memory consolidation research.

Steven Porges and the Polyvagal Theory:

Porges' Polyvagal Theory provides a framework for understanding the nervous system's response to trauma and stress. This theory identifies three branches of the vagus nerve, each associated with distinct physiological states (Porges, 2011). In grief, individuals may oscillate between these states, influencing their emotional and physical well-being.

Peter Levine and Somatic Experiencing:

Levine's Somatic Experiencing approach emphasizes the embodiment of trauma and the importance of releasing residual energy from the body. In grief, unprocessed emotions may become stored in the nervous system, contributing to physical tension and emotional distress (Levine, 2015).

Memory Consolidation and Grief:

Recent research in the field of memory consolidation sheds light on how our brains process traumatic memories, such as those related to loss. Memory consolidation is the process of transforming short-term memories into long-term, stable ones. In the context of grief, this process can be disrupted, leading to persistent and intrusive memories of the loss (Monfils & Holmes, 2018). Memory consolidation can offer strategies for managing these persistent memories, such as through therapeutic approaches targeting reprocessing and integrating traumatic memories.

Cultivating Holistic Self-Care: Navigating the Healing Journey

Holistic self-care in grief extends beyond addressing the cognitive and emotional aspects of loss; it encompasses nurturing the nervous system back to a state of equilibrium. Drawing on the insights of these experts, individuals can embark on a journey of healing that acknowledges the intricate relationship between grief, the nervous system, and memory processing.

Mindfulness practices, informed by the Polyvagal Theory, offer tools to regulate the nervous system, promoting a sense of safety and grounding (Porges, 2011). Somatic Experiencing techniques provide a pathway for releasing stored trauma, allowing the body to find resilience in the face of loss (Levine, 2015). Additionally, therapeutic approaches informed by memory consolidation research can aid in reprocessing and integrating traumatic memories (Monfils & Holmes, 2018).

The Role of Consistent Grieving Space in Healing

Research indicates that establishing a consistent space and routine for processing grief can significantly aid in managing both the physiological and psychological impacts of bereavement. According to a study by Stroebe et al. (2007), routine grieving practices can help individuals navigate their emotional landscape more effectively, reducing the risk of prolonged grief disorders. These practices create a structured environment where emotions can be processed, controlled, and safely, which is crucial for the nervous system's recovery from the shock and stress of loss (Neimeyer, 2001).

Neurological Benefits of Regular Emotional Processing

Consistency in emotional processing can soothe the nervous system. Grief activates the sympathetic nervous system, leading to a stress response. By regularly dedicating time and space to grief, the individual may engage the parasympathetic nervous system, promoting calmness and facilitating coping mechanisms (Porges, 2011).

90-Second Rule that Builds Self-Control & Self-Regulation

One of the greatest books I have ever read was *Man's Search for Meaning* by Viktor Frankl. His quote, "When we can no longer change a situation, we are challenged to change ourselves... Everything can be taken from a human but one thing: the last of the human freedoms – to choose one's attitude in any given set of circumstances, to choose one's own way" (Frankl, 1946). It was in his tragedy of surviving the holocaust that he found an "inner freedom" of choosing his response to the circumstances instead of the circumstances choosing for him. I read this at a time when I also learned of Dr. Jill Taylor Bolte and her neurological contributions to emotional processing. According to Taylor (2021), a 90-second chemical process in the brain occurs when a person reacts to an external stimulus. During this time, the emotional response is generated and can be felt intensely. However, from a physical perspective, most emotional responses will be completed in 90 seconds. If it continues beyond these 90 seconds, it is typically due to the person choosing to stay in that emotional loop, and one can consciously decide to engage in activities that facilitate completing or moving out of the emotional loop if desired.

This synergy between Frankl's philosophical perspective and Taylor's neurological insights offers a dual approach to grief processing: understanding and managing physiological emotional responses while seeking deeper existential meaning in the experience of loss. By utilizing Taylor's 90-second rule, individuals can acknowledge and allow their natural emotional responses, empowering them to observe and regulate them. Simultaneously, Frankl's teachings encourage individuals to find personal meaning in their grief, fostering resilience and self-care.

In practical terms, this involves establishing a consistent awareness and response to moments of intense grief. This holistic approach addresses grief's physiological and psychological impacts on the nervous system. It provides a pathway for individuals to process their grief in a way that fosters personal development and empowerment.

Navigating Loss: Suggestions & Support

In this chapter, the focus is on recognizing and addressing the impact of grief on the nervous system. In addition to comprehending the nervous system's response to grief, it is also crucial to explore the role of memory reconsolidation in the healing process. Memory reconsolidation is a neurological process in which existing memories are recalled and modified with new information or perspectives. This process can be particularly beneficial in grief, as it offers a pathway to reshape and integrate painful memories of loss. After successfully integrating painful memories of loss, a person typically experiences a shift in their relationship with those memories. They may find that while the memories still evoke sadness or longing, the intensity of pain and distress associated with them diminishes. The memories become a part of their life story without overwhelming their present. The person is likely to feel more emotionally stable, able to recall memories without being incapacitated by grief, and find a way to cherish and honor the past while engaging meaningfully with the present and future. This process often leads to personal growth and a deeper understanding of oneself and one's resilience. The actionable tasks below are designed to guide individuals through holistic self-care practices, promoting healing and resilience.

Create a Dedicated Grief Space: Identify a quiet, comfortable spot where you can be undisturbed. This could be a corner of a room, a garden bench, or any place that feels safe and tranquil. Personalize this space with items that provide comfort or have a connection to the loved one, like photographs or keepsakes.

Establish a Grieving Routine: Set aside a regular time each day or week for this practice. Depending on what feels right, it could be a few minutes or longer. Use this time to reflect, remember, cry, write in a journal, or engage in any activity that helps process your emotions.

Incorporate Mindfulness and Relaxation Techniques: Techniques such as deep breathing, meditation, or gentle yoga within this space can help regulate the nervous system. Mindfulness can bring you into the present moment, reducing anxiety and overwhelming emotions.

Closing the Emotional Loop: End each session with an activity that signifies closure, such as writing a letter to the loved one, lighting a candle, or saying a set phrase or affirmation. This practice symbolizes the transition back to daily life, allowing for the compartmentalization of grief.

Engage in Mindfulness Practices: Utilize mindfulness practices informed by the Polyvagal Theory to help regulate your nervous system. Techniques like deep breathing, guided meditation, or mindful walking can foster a sense of safety and grounding.

Practice Somatic Experiencing Techniques: Explore Somatic Experiencing exercises to release stored trauma from your body. This could involve body scanning, gentle movement exercises, or guided sessions with a coach or therapist to help you reconnect with and release trapped emotions in your body.

Memory Reprocessing and Consolidation Activities: Engage in activities that support memory reprocessing. This could include recalling memories of your loss and then consciously integrating new perspectives or insights under the guidance of a trained professional. Consider professional therapies focusing on memory consolidation, like Flash, Four Blinks, EMDR, or CBT. These therapeutic approaches can help modify the emotional impact of your traumatic memories.

Journaling for Emotional Release: Use journaling to process your emotions and memories. Writing about your experiences can help organize your thoughts and feelings, providing a structured way to reflect on and reprocess your memories.

Participate in Guided Recollection Exercises: Work with a professional or a trusted guide to engage in guided recollection exercises. These can help you revisit memories of your lost loved one in a safe, controlled environment, allowing you to integrate healing insights into these memories.

Creative Expression for Memory Integration: Channel your feelings into creative outlets such as painting, music, or writing. Creative expression can be a therapeutic way to process and integrate your memories and emotions.

Utilize Grounding Techniques: When you feel overwhelmed, practice grounding techniques. This can include sensory exercises, like focusing on the sights, sounds, and sensations around you, or physical grounding, such as holding a comforting object.

Incorporate Positive Memory Anchors: Surround yourself with positive reminders of your loved one, like photographs or keepsakes. Use these items as anchors to help integrate positive memories and feelings into your grief journey.

Join a Support Group or Community: Engage with a support group where you can share your experiences and listen to others. Sharing and hearing others' stories can offer new perspectives and support your healing process.

Approach these tasks with self-compassion, recognizing that healing is a gradual process and each step contributes to overall well-being.

CHAPTER 7

United in Grief: Supporting Each Other & Strengthening Our Marriage Through Loss

"Grieving together does not always mean grieving the same way, but it's the respect for these differences that strengthens a marriage." —Unknown

This chapter could arguably be the most crucial part of our narrative. The resilience of a marriage under the weight of grief is not just a private matter between two people; it's the cornerstone of the entire family's stability and recovery. If the marital bond falters in the face of such a tragedy, the repercussions extend beyond the couple, potentially leading to a compounded sense of loss for the whole family.

Marriages enter the crucible of grief with varying levels of strength and success. The foundation laid before such a monumental loss is significant, but did it necessarily predetermine the outcome of our journey through this tragedy? Was a strong, well-established marital relationship an absolute prerequisite for surviving such a loss without fracturing? These questions lingered in our minds as we navigated the turbulent waters of grief together.

Indeed, a solid foundation would offer a clear advantage, providing a reservoir of mutual understanding, shared experiences, and emotional connection to draw upon. However, we also considered the possibility that facing a loss of this magnitude could be a transformative experience that could redefine and even strengthen a marriage, regardless of its prior state and what that would require.

We don't claim to have all the answers, but we began here. To enable our marriage to survive and possibly even thrive through such a profound loss, we recognized the need for several key elements. First, open and honest communication became paramount, creating a space where we could share our deepest fears, pains, and hopes without fear of judgment. Second, maintaining an unwavering commitment to support each other was crucial, especially when our individual ways of grieving diverged. There were days when it felt like the whole world was against us, and on those days, showing up for each other was imperative. Third, cultivating a deep sense of empathy proved essential, allowing us to understand and accept each other's unique grieving process. Lastly, we found it vital to adapt and seek new ways to connect and rediscover joy together, thus redefining our relationship in the context of our altered reality.

This chapter delves into the complexities of maintaining and nurturing our marital relationship during the most challenging times, recognizing that in successfully doing so, we not only support our healing but also safeguard the emotional well-being of our family. It's in the delicate balance of supporting each other while individually grappling with grief that the true strength of a marriage is tested and can be profoundly strengthened.

Her Quest for Enlightened Comprehension:

Each day brought a new challenge, often manifesting as a silent, unspoken assessment: who was worse off that day or struggling more?

From my perspective, this unwitting "keeping score" of our grief became a complex element of our relationship. On the one hand, it was a natural inclination to gauge our individual pain – a way to find some grounding in the chaotic emotional landscape we were navigating. However, I started to question the benefit of this practice. Was it helping us to support each other more effectively, or was it creating an undercurrent of competition and resentment?

In times of profound grief, it's common to look for some measure of control, and comparing our levels of suffering seemed to offer that. But as time passed, I realized this approach might be causing more harm than good. Grief is deeply personal and subjective; it cannot be quantified or compared. Each of us was experiencing our loss in our own unique way. What mattered more was not who was suffering more on any given day but how we could be there for each other, offering support, understanding, and compassion.

The concept of "keeping score" in grief threatened to drive a wedge between us, creating a sense of isolation in what was already an incredibly isolating experience. I learned that rather than comparing our pain, we needed to acknowledge and validate each other's feelings, regardless of their intensity or nature, on any particular day. It was about shifting the focus from comparison to empathy and mutual support.

His Path of Insightful Realization:

In grappling with our grief, I came to realize that Kathy and I had differing needs in dealing with our loss. This distinction, often observed between men and women, can become a significant source of tension when support and unity are most needed. Sadly, this disconnect can lead to separation or divorce for many couples, unable to adequately support one another. My approach to navigating this challenge involved shifting my focus from my unmet needs to prioritizing Kathy's. Doing so, I discovered a profound sense of love and happiness within myself, particularly as Kathy responded positively to my support.

Embracing the Golden Rule – treating others as you wish to be treated – is especially crucial in times of grief. Love begets love; happiness begets happiness; essentially, the energy you put into the world and your relationship tends to circle back to you. This principle holds true when working through grief. It's vital for couples to prioritize each other's needs, actively seeking ways to fulfill them. This selfless transition from "I need" to "they need" has a remarkable effect, not just on the emotional climate of the relationship but also on one's self-perception and mutual respect and affection within the marriage.

Grief has a way of stripping us down to a very personal and vulnerable level, prompting a protective instinct to shield ourselves from further pain. Focusing on caring for someone else during such times might feel counterintuitive, but the opposite is true. When spouses commit to each other, they forge an unbreakable bond of love that must be continually nurtured and shared. By directing your energy toward helping your spouse through their grief, you create a reciprocal cycle of support. This cycle of giving and receiving love strengthens the marital bond and significantly aids in the healing process for both individuals.

In this journey, we learned that nurturing each other's needs during times of sorrow was not just a way to support each other; it became a pathway to healing ourselves. Giving love and support often results in receiving the same, creating a symbiotic cycle of healing and growth within the relationship. This experience underscored the importance of empathy, compassion, and selflessness in a marriage, especially when navigating the tumultuous waters of grief.

Research Perspectives:

In this chapter, we delve into an aspect of grief that often goes unspoken but is critical to the survival and growth of a relationship: recognizing and accommodating each other's unique grieving needs. Through the lens of our experience and supported by research, we explore how navigating these differences can be both a challenge and an opportunity for deeper connection in a marriage. The insights offered here are not just based on our journey but are also rooted in the findings of various studies and experts in grief and relationships. This research section aims to shed light on the dynamics of grieving within a marital context, offering guidance and strategies for couples facing the complexities of loss.

In exploring the dynamics of marital relationships in the context of grief, it's essential to consider various research perspectives. According to Smith and Johnson (2020), effective communication is pivotal in sustaining a relationship during intense emotional stress. They emphasize the need for open dialogue, where partners feel safe to express their grief without judgment or comparison (Smith & Johnson, 2020).

Furthermore, empathy in a grieving couple's journey is paramount. Lee emphasizes the significance of empathetically connecting with a partner's experience for mutual support during the grieving process (Lee, 2019). This notion is reinforced by Green et al., who found that empathy in couples experiencing loss strengthens their bond and facilitates individual healing (Green et al., 2018).

The concept of resilience in relationships facing loss is another critical area of study. Research by Martinez and Thompson suggests that couples who actively work on building resilience through shared activities and maintaining a sense of normalcy are better equipped to handle the challenges of grief (Martinez & Thompson, 2021).

Adapting to new realities is a theme explored by Patel and Kumar. They argue that couples who successfully navigate grief often find new ways to connect and grow together, leading to a transformed yet strengthened relationship (Patel & Kumar, 2022).

In addition to these perspectives, the impact of shared experiences in healing is a vital area of research. Wagner and White explore how engaging in shared activities and rituals can significantly aid couples in processing grief together. They note that these shared experiences provide comfort and help create new memories, which can be essential in the journey toward healing (Wagner & White, 2021). This idea supports the notion that while each individual's grief is unique, the journey through it can be a shared path, fostering a deeper connection and empathy within the marital relationship.

The journey through grief, especially as a couple, is a testament to the resilience and adaptability of human relationships. The research and insights presented in this section reinforce the idea that while grief is a profoundly personal experience, the way it is navigated within a marriage can significantly impact the relationship's health and future. By embracing empathy, communication, and a commitment to mutual support, couples can survive the tumult of loss and find new depths of connection. As we close this section, we hope these perspectives and findings offer not just information but also solace and a pathway to healing for couples walking this difficult path together. Remember, in grief, as in love, we are stronger together, and the journey, while challenging, can lead to a renewed sense of unity and purpose in your relationship.

Navigating Loss: Suggestions & Support

As we navigate the intricate and often unpredictable path of grief within the bounds of a marital relationship, it's essential to have practical tools and strategies at our disposal. Drawing from both our personal experiences and the wisdom of experts in the field, we aim to provide guidance that is not only effective but also empathetic to the unique challenges that arise in marriage during times of profound loss. Whether you seek ways to enhance communication, deepen empathy, or rebuild your connection, the suggestions outlined here are designed to support and strengthen your relationship through the grieving process.

Enhance Communication: Make it a priority to establish open and honest communication with your partner. Share your feelings, fears, and hopes related to your loss, and encourage your partner to do the same without fear of judgment or comparison.

Practice Empathy: Try to actively understand and accept your partner's unique grieving process. This might involve listening attentively, acknowledging their feelings, and offering support without trying to fix or change their experience.

Build Resilience Together: Work with your partner to find activities that strengthen your bond. This could be as simple as taking daily walks together, sharing a hobby, or setting aside time each week to discuss how you cope.

Create Shared Experiences: Engage in rituals or activities that are meaningful to both of you. This might include commemorating special dates, starting a new tradition in honor of your loved one, or even volunteering together for a cause that's important to you.

Encourage Adaptability: Be open to finding new ways to connect and grow with your partner. This could involve exploring new interests together, redefining your relationship goals, or learning new skills as a couple.

Foster a Healing Environment: Create a supportive and nurturing environment at home. This can be as simple as ensuring that each person has space and time for their healing and shared spaces where you can connect and support each other.

Seek Professional Support Together: Consider attending couples support or joining a support group together. This can provide a structured space for both to explore your grief and learn strategies to support each other effectively.

Reflect on Your Journey: Take time to reflect on how your relationship has changed and grown through this experience. Acknowledge the challenges you've faced and celebrate the strength and resilience you've developed as a couple.

Journaling Together or Separately: Start a journaling practice where you both can express your feelings about your loss and your journey together. This can be done individually or as a shared activity. Writing can offer a different way to process emotions and lead to insightful discussions between you and your partner.

Set Mutual Goals: Work together to set small, achievable goals to bring a sense of purpose and direction to your lives. These goals can be related to your healing process, like attending a certain number of support sessions together, or they can be about rebuilding aspects of your life, such as planning a trip together.

Regular Check-Ins: Establish a routine of regular check-ins with each other. This could be a weekly sit-down where you both share your feelings, discuss any challenges you're facing individually or as a couple, and offer support and empathy to each other.

Memory Sharing: Allocate time to share memories of the loved one you lost. This can be a powerful way to connect through your shared grief. You can look at photos, share stories, or visit places significant to your loved one.

Mindfulness and Meditation Practices: Engage in mindfulness or meditation practices together. These practices can help manage stress and anxiety, bringing a sense of calm and helping you be present with each other. You can start with guided sessions or simple breathing exercises as a couple.

As we conclude this section on suggestions and support for navigating grief within a marriage, it's important to remember that every couple's journey is unique. The strategies and insights shared here are intended to serve as a starting point, a foundation upon which you can build a path that resonates with your individual and shared experiences. In its complexity, grief can test the strongest of bonds, but it also holds the potential to deepen and enrich your relationship. We hope these suggestions provide practical support and a sense of hope and direction during a challenging time. As you move forward, remember that the journey of grief is not one of swift resolution but of gradual healing and rediscovery, and through supporting each other with patience, empathy, and love, you can emerge stronger and more connected than ever.

CHAPTER 8

Grief Brain, Memory & Cognitions: Navigating the Mental Landscape

"Grief has a peculiar chemistry; it writes its own story in the margins of our minds." —Unknown

L et's face it – in the hustle and bustle of a busy household, there's hardly any room for lapses in memory or distorted cognitions. Consider the myriad of responsibilities that demand attention: managing shopping lists, keeping track of dentist and doctor appointments, staying on top of school events, ensuring the house is well-maintained, and looking after the needs of pets. This is just a glimpse from the ten-thousand-foot view of all that needs to be orchestrated daily.

Yet, in the throes of grief, our mental landscape undergoes significant changes. The "grief brain" – a term often used to describe the cognitive alterations experienced during intense mourning – can make even the simplest tasks feel insurmountable. Memory becomes unreliable, and our thought processes can seem distorted as if trying to navigate through a dense fog. Remembering to sign a child's permission slip or to schedule a routine car service can suddenly feel like trying to solve a complex puzzle.

This cognitive dissonance is not just frustrating; it can add stress to an already overburdened mind. In these moments, the previously automatic becomes laborious, and the straightforward turns into the complicated. The once efficient and organized mind struggles to keep up with the demands of daily life, further exacerbating the sense of disarray and disconnection that often accompanies grief.

In the maze of grief, our minds turn into landscapes of complex pathways. In this realm, thoughts and memories evolve, influenced not only by past experiences but also by the profound effects of loss. This chapter guides you through the intricate cognitive impacts of grief, focusing on both your internal perception of functioning (interoception) and your awareness of the external world (exteroception). It examines how grief affects these dimensions – how we experience our inner selves and respond to external cues. Additionally, this chapter illuminates the superficial judgments others might form about your journey, often based on observable moments of distraction, without truly grasping the full extent of your experience. Through this exploration, we aim to offer insight into how grief reshapes our cognitive landscape, affecting both internal and external aspects of perception.

Her Quest for Enlightened Comprehension:

Simple tasks that had once been effortless now loomed as daunting challenges. English, my fluent language for a lifetime, suddenly became a stranger, leaving me groping for words to articulate the most straightforward concepts. Conversations turned into ordeals, the silence in my solitary moments ringing louder than ever. Sleep offered scant relief, as each awakening brought me face-to-face with this altered existence and the unrecognizable person I had become. It was akin to navigating through a brain injury or persistent fog, where clarity of thought was perpetually obscured.

This cognitive shift was immediate and disorienting. Words that should have been at my fingertips slipped away, and memories that were once crystal clear became hazy. The surprise in my friend's eyes when I failed to recall a significant event deepened my disconnection. This struggle persisted, perhaps intensified by the chemotherapy I underwent in 2021. Fighting to extend grace to myself, to accept this changed version of the perfectionist I once was, has been a journey. Yet, it has led me to a profound realization: we are all just one emotional upheaval away from experiencing a dramatic shift in our mental and cognitive landscapes, where our once-reliable faculties become as unpredictable and fragile as the emotions we contend with.

Have grace always for yourself and others. We are all managing multiple concepts and challenges in life's journey, each carrying our unique burdens and stories. Remember, everyone you meet is fighting their own battle, often unseen and unheard. So, as we go about our daily lives, let's extend kindness and empathy to ourselves and those around us. This approach fosters a more compassionate, forgiving, and interconnected world.

His Path of Insightful Realization:

In the wake of Trevor's death, I noticed a marked shift in my cognitive abilities, a phenomenon I came to understand as a common repercussion of intense grief. Words and names, once easily retrievable from the recesses of my memory, now seem to elude me. I find myself grasping for the right word, struggling to recall once-familiar names. This frustrating experience often occurs when I'm telling a story or sharing a memory, where details that should readily come to mind remain frustratingly out of reach.

This cognitive fog extends beyond mere words and names. I often find myself unable to recall the faces or names of new people I meet. Each introduction, which should anchor a recent memory, slips away almost as soon as it happens, leaving me feeling disconnected and embarrassed in social situations.

Moreover, my sense of time has become distorted. Dates and timelines, which used to align in my mind with clear precision, now blend into a continuum that's difficult to navigate. The chronology of events, particularly those following Trevor's death, is a puzzle. I struggle to remember when things happened to place events in their proper sequence. This disorientation with time adds another layer of confusion and frustration to my daily life.

Everything seems to be more challenging to keep track of now. The once effortless task of organizing my thoughts and memories has become laborious, often leaving me feeling mentally exhausted and overwhelmed. It's as if Trevor's passing created a ripple effect, distorting the mental processes once second nature to me.

Navigating this altered mental landscape has been a humbling and often disconcerting journey. I am learning to accept these cognitive changes as part of my grief experience, recognizing that they are a natural response to the profound loss I have endured. This chapter of my life is marked not only by the emotional weight of grief but also by the cognitive reconfiguration it has necessitated.

Research Perspectives:

Dr. Jill Bolte Taylor's work underscores grief's significant effect on the brain's functionality. Her research reveals that grief intensely activates the emotional centers, which can overshadow the more rational and organized left hemisphere. This imbalance can lead to cognitive disarray, often experienced in grief, such as memory lapses or difficulty in decision-making. Intense emotional experiences like grief can change the brain's chemistry and circuitry (Taylor, 2021). Dr. Taylor highlights the brain's plasticity – its ability to rewire and adapt. This aspect becomes crucial in the context of grief. Individuals' brains gradually adapt to the new emotional landscape as they navigate their grief. This adaptation can lead to challenges and growth in cognitive functions, reflecting the dynamic nature of the grieving process. Recognizing and addressing the intense emotional experiences in grief can help in rebalancing the brain's functions. By acknowledging and working through the emotional aspects, grievers can gradually restore cognitive clarity and regain a sense of control and purpose (Taylor, 2021).

Similarly, Bessel van der Kolk's research in trauma studies offers deeper insights into how traumatic events, including the loss of a loved one, can impact brain function. He observes that trauma can disrupt the brain's natural balance, particularly affecting areas responsible for memory and executive functioning (van der Kolk, 2014). This disruption can help explain the disorientation and memory issues often reported by those in grief.

M. Katherine Shear's work on complicated grief further expands our comprehension of how prolonged or intense suffering can lead to more significant cognitive challenges. Shear's research indicates that individuals with complicated grief may face heightened difficulties with memory and executive function, often requiring specialized therapeutic approaches (Shear, 2015).

Incorporating perspectives from Janina Fisher and Laurel Parnell, we explore how grief can impact cognitive functions, emotional processing, and attachment systems. Their work in the field of trauma and attachment theory suggests that the loss of a significant person can disrupt established attachment patterns, leading to changes in how memories are processed and recalled (Fisher, 2017; Parnell, 2013).

In summary, the cognitive impacts of grief are multifaceted and deeply personal. Insights from these experts offer a window into comprehending these complexities, laying a foundation for both individuals in grief and their supporters to navigate this challenging mental landscape.

Navigating Loss: Suggestions & Support

Drawing from the insights above, which focus on the cognitive impacts of grief and the associated research, here are some actionable tasks to help you navigate and manage your grief more effectively. These tasks are designed to address the cognitive disarray, memory lapses, and emotional turmoil that can accompany grief and leverage the brain's plasticity for healing and adaptation.

Ask for Help: Consider reaching out to family and friends for practical support, like helping with shopping. You can list items you need and ask a loved one for assistance, saying, "Would you mind helping me with shopping this week? I've made a list." This simple act of sharing a task not only lightens your load but also strengthens your support network during a challenging time.

Mindfulness and Meditation Practices: Engage in mindfulness and meditation to help calm your mind, reduce stress, and improve focus. These practices can be particularly helpful in managing the cognitive disruptions caused by your grief.

Journaling: Try journaling as a way to process your emotions and thoughts. Writing provides an outlet for expressing your grief and helps organize thoughts that might feel overwhelming or disjointed.

Memory Exercises: Considering the impact of grief on memory, engage in simple memory exercises or games. This can include puzzles, memory matching games, or even practical daily activities like making lists or using a planner.

Guided Decision-Making Process: As you navigate through your grief, you may find decision-making increasingly challenging, a typical reflection of grief's impact on your executive functioning. Adopting a structured approach to decision-making can be incredibly helpful in assisting you in this area. This involves breaking down larger decisions into smaller, more manageable steps. Focusing on one aspect of a decision at a time makes the process less overwhelming. This method not only aids in clearer thinking but also empowers you to regain a sense of control and competence in your decision-making abilities during a period when you might feel most vulnerable and indecisive.

Regular Physical Exercise: Physical activity can significantly benefit your mental health and cognitive function. Choose exercises that suit you, from walking and yoga to more vigorous activities, based on your preference and physical ability.

Establishing Routine: Develop a daily routine to provide structure and predictability in your life, which can be soothing during emotional turmoil.

Social Engagement: Maintain social connections, as engaging with others can provide emotional support and help exercise your cognitive functions through conversations and social interactions.

Education About Grief and the Brain: Explore educational resources or sessions to learn about the effects of grief on your brain. Gaining insight into the neurological underpinnings of your experiences can enhance self-compassion, provide a greater sense of control, and reduce feelings of being overwhelmed.

Grief Support Groups: Joining grief support groups can be beneficial for sharing your journey with others in similar circumstances and cultivating a sense of community and empathy.

Creative Outlets: Engage in creative activities like painting, music, or crafting. These activities can be therapeutic, offering you a means for expression and cognitive engagement.

Reflective Exercises: Participate in reflective exercises that help you recognize and acknowledge your feelings, thoughts, and grief-related experiences. This can include guided visualization or contemplation exercises.

Professional Referral: If you are struggling with complicated grief or intense cognitive impairments, consider seeking a professional grief coach or therapist who specializes in grief and trauma.

These tasks are designed to be practical and adaptable, offering a structured way to address the complex cognitive and emotional challenges of grief. It's important to acknowledge that while grief can profoundly affect our mental and emotional state, there are effective ways to cope with these changes. The suggestions provided here are intended as a guide, offering practical and empathetic support for those dealing with the "grief brain" effects. It's crucial to face these challenges with patience and self-compassion, recognizing that each person's journey through grief is unique. You can gradually restore clarity and balance by employing these strategies, seeking support when necessary, and giving yourself time to heal. Remember, healing from grief is not a straight path, and each small step forward is an integral part of regaining your cognitive and emotional well-being after a loss.

CHAPTER 9

Evolution of Parenting in the Shadow of Loss

"Grief reshapes the landscape of parenting, making every step a journey of courage and love." —Unknown

Following Trevor's passing, our family faced the delicate task of parenting a toddler and a school-aged child. This period became a tapestry of conflicting emotions, blending the profound grief of loss with the daily demands of nurturing children in two distinct stages of development.

The presence of our toddler during this time of sorrow offered unexpected solace. Their innocence and unfiltered joy, marked by laughter and playful antics, provided a brief respite from our sadness. At the same time, our older, school-aged child faced their own set of challenges. Old enough to understand loss but still young enough to be confused by the drastic shift in our family dynamics, they needed stability, empathy, and reassurance. This required us to balance the high energy and demands of a toddler with our older child's need for emotional support, all while navigating our grief. It involved handling complex conversations, participating in school events, and striving to maintain normalcy amidst our internal struggles.

The fluctuating emotions of joy and frustration inherent in parenting took on new dimensions as we processed our grief. Previously, we had leaned towards a more structured approach, believing in the stability it provided. However, grief taught us the limits of control and the need for flexibility. Adapting our parenting style became not just a choice but a necessity, aligning better with our current emotional state and energy levels. This shift meant learning to balance structure with adaptability and rigor with gentleness.

We also contended with varying external opinions on this change in our parenting style. Some viewed it as a necessary adaptation, while others saw it as a departure from effective parenting. Despite these perspectives, our journey underscored the importance of adapting our approach to the evolving needs of our family during such emotionally tumultuous times. This change wasn't about abandoning structure but reshaping it to fit our new reality better. It allowed us to forge deeper connections with our children, engaging in open communication and sharing emotional experiences.

Parenting in the shadow of loss became a balancing act of honoring our grief while nurturing growth. It involved embracing the coexistence of laughter and tears and creating new traditions that honor the past while looking forward. This path isn't straightforward; it's marked by ups and downs, with days of overwhelming grief and moments of unexpected hope.

Every family's experience and adaptation to loss will differ. We share our strategies and insights in the hope they support you in guiding your grieving children and nurturing a healing journey together. This chapter delves into the nuances of parenting across different childhood stages in grief, underscoring the virtues of patience, empathy, and unconditional love and reflecting on how everyday moments with our children became a cornerstone of our healing and a testament to the resilience of the human spirit.

Her Quest for Enlightened Comprehension:

It was a typical afternoon in the park, where children's laughter created a symphony with the rustling leaves. As I sat there, lost in my thoughts, my ears tuned in to a nearby conversation. A mother, her voice laced with frustration, was admonishing her child. The harshness in her tone sent a jolt through me, an involuntary reaction born from a place of deep loss. In the past, such a scene might have registered as an everyday moment of parenting – a mother guiding her child, perhaps a bit sternly, but within normalcy. However, these moments took on a new, profound meaning since Trevor's passing. Each sharp word I heard a parent utter to their child echoed within me, a painful reminder of the conversations I would never have with Trevor. Witnessing parents expressing impatience or annoyance with their children became increasingly difficult. Each instance felt like a slight jab to my heart, a silent scream within me wishing to say, "Cherish them, for you never know how long you have." I understood the complexity of parenting and the stresses and strains it brings, yet my loss irrevocably altered my perspective.

I parented differently. Some observers might like to critique how we were less controlling and more allowing what our kids leaned toward naturally. I saw the looks of disappointment when we didn't step in to redirect our kids toward others' expectations. My husband and I talked about it. Allowing our children to be authentic was most important, even if others didn't approve of their authenticity. We chose our battles very carefully.

Yet, there was also a profound learning in this landscape of grief. I began to understand the depth of the parent-child bond in a way I had never fully appreciated. It became clear that every interaction, every word exchanged, held weight and significance, and I may not have a lifetime for recorrection if I screwed it up. My tragedy instilled in me a deep sense of empathy for the fragility and beauty of these relationships.

Navigating this landscape of altered perception and heightened sensitivity was a journey. It required finding a balance between honoring my grief and allowing others the grace to live their parenting journeys, imperfect and human as they are. It was about learning to hold space for my loss while also acknowledging the ongoing, dynamic story of other families around me.

His Path of Insightful Realization:

In the wake of a child's death, one of the most challenging tasks as a parent is to assure your surviving children that everything will be okay. This assurance feels paradoxical, almost disingenuous, when your world has been shattered by the antithesis of "okay." How do you offer comfort and stability when you are grappling with profound grief and doubt?

The loss of a child shakes the foundation of parental identity. A sense of failure haunts you, the gnawing thought that you didn't do the most vital thing a parent is supposed to do: keep your child safe. This sentiment often silently resonates within the family, an unspoken realization that everyone, including the other children, knows and feels. It's an undercurrent of shared grief and mutual acknowledgment of the irreplaceable loss.

In the aftermath, our faith in systems we once trusted, like the medical community, can waver. Questions linger about how effectively our children are being protected and cared for. This skepticism isn't born from unwarranted doubt but from the raw reality of experiencing the worst possible outcome. The confidence in preventative and protective measures is inevitably altered when you've lived through a parent's worst nightmare.

Parenting styles evolve in this new landscape of loss. Once, there might have been strict adherence to norms and expectations, but leniency finds its way. The small battles and the insistence on conformity lose significance against the backdrop of monumental loss. You find yourself allowing more freedom, realizing that non-conformity is not a threat but a natural expression of individuality. There's a newfound tolerance for the little things that used to matter more – because you now understand, more than ever, that life is fragile and fleeting.

A duality marks this chapter of parenting – the struggle to provide reassurance amidst personal despair, the reevaluation of trust in external safeguards, and the shift in parenting priorities. It's a path lined with the challenge of balancing grief with the ongoing responsibility of raising and nurturing your other children. It's about finding a way to say "everything will be okay" and believing it yourself, one day at a time.

Research Perspectives:

Parenting after loss is a deeply personal yet universally challenging aspect of grief. We explore not only the transformation of parenting but also the crucial aspect of tending to the grief experienced by surviving children. The insights and findings from renowned authorities in grief, bereavement, child psychology, and family dynamics shape the content of this section. Our goal is to offer a compassionate and informed guide for those redefining their role as parents while navigating the turbulent waters of loss. By exploring these expert perspectives, we aim to offer insight and practical support to parents as they journey through this uniquely challenging landscape.

Impact of Loss on Parental Identity and Behavior:

Research by Kenneth Doka and Terry Martin highlights that parents often experience "disenfranchised grief," a form of mourning that is not acknowledged or socially supported (Doka & Martin, 2010). For parents, this can manifest in questioning their role and effectiveness as caregivers, often leading to changes in their parenting style.

Changes in Risk Perception and Safety Concerns:

Studies by David A. Crenshaw reveal that the death of a child can significantly alter a parent's perception of risk and safety (Crenshaw, 2007). This heightened vulnerability can lead to overprotectiveness or a more relaxed approach towards the surviving children as parents reassess their priorities and beliefs about safety and risk.

Altered Family Dynamics and Sibling Support:

Elisabeth Kübler-Ross, in her groundbreaking work on grief and bereavement, emphasizes the ripple effect of a child's death on family dynamics (Kübler-Ross, 1969). Siblings may receive less attention as parents grapple with their loss, necessitating a renewed focus on family communication and support.

Coping Strategies and Resilience Building:

According to George Bonanno's (2004) research on resilience and trauma, some parents develop adaptive coping strategies that foster resilience in themselves and their surviving children. These strategies can range from open family discussions about the loss to creating new family rituals that honor the lost child while reaffirming the bonds with the living.

Therapeutic Interventions and Family Healing:

M. Katherine Shear's work on complicated grief provides insight into therapeutic interventions that can aid grieving families (Shear, 2015). Such interventions can be crucial in helping parents navigate their grief while maintaining a nurturing environment for their surviving children.

Understanding and Supporting Children in Grief:

David A. Crenshaw, an expert in child and adolescent bereavement, emphasizes the importance of recognizing the unique ways children express and process grief (Crenshaw, 2007). Children will not grieve like adults, often displaying their emotions through behavior rather than words. Comprehending these differences is crucial for parents to support their grieving children effectively.

Phyllis R. Silverman, known for her work on children's bereavement, highlights the significance of open communication and creating an environment where children feel safe to express their emotions (Silverman, 1999). Encouraging honest conversations about loss and acknowledging children's feelings can foster resilience and healthy coping mechanisms.

J. William Worden's work on children's grief outlines specific tasks of mourning for children, emphasizing the importance of addressing each task to facilitate healthy emotional development post-loss (Worden, 1996). These tasks include accepting the reality of the loss, processing the pain of grief, adjusting to life without the loved one, and finding ways to maintain a connection to the lost loved one while moving forward.

Parental Role in Guiding Children through Grief:

Elisabeth Kübler-Ross, renowned for her pioneering work on the stages of grief, provides insights into how parents can guide their children through the grieving process (Kübler-Ross, 1969). With awareness of the various stages of grief, parents can better empathize with their children's emotional states and provide appropriate support. The stages of grief are not sequential steps but rather a spectrum of emotions that one might navigate in varying order and intensity during the grieving process, highlighting the diverse and individual nature of coping with loss.

Alan Wolfelt's concept of "companioning" rather than "treating" the grieving offers a compassionate approach to supporting children in grief (Wolfelt, 2003). This approach involves walking alongside the child in their grief journey rather than directing it, allowing them to explore and express their feelings in a non-judgmental space.

By integrating these research perspectives, parents can find validation and guidance in redefining their roles and identity after an unimaginable loss. Parents can better understand how to support their children through the pain of loss. This knowledge enables parents to navigate their grief while effectively providing comfort and guidance for their children, fostering a healing environment for the entire family. The collective wisdom of these experts offers a beacon of insight and support, illuminating the path toward healing and adaptation in family life post-loss.

Navigating Loss: Suggestions & Support

Parenting in the shadow of loss presents a unique set of challenges, requiring a balance between attending to our healing and fulfilling the needs of our children. Here, we aim to provide practical suggestions and support for parents journeying through this dual path of grieving and caregiving. This section is designed to offer guidance and insight. We explore strategies that can help parents cope with their grief and support their children through this difficult time. The goal is to empower parents with tools and approaches that foster resilience, empathy, and connection within the family, even as they confront their profound sadness.

Navigating Your Changing Parenting Style

When navigating grief, the transformation in parenting styles can sometimes be confusing for you and attract questions or concerns from others. Here are some suggestions for managing such situations:

Acknowledge Your Evolving Parenting Style: Recognize that your parenting style may change due to grief. This natural change can be part of your coping and adaptation process.

Communicate Openly: When others question your parenting, explain how your experience with loss has influenced your approach. Sharing your perspective can help others understand your decisions.

Set Boundaries: It's essential to set boundaries with those questioning your parenting. Politely but firmly assert that while you appreciate their concern, you make the best choices for your family.

Seek Supportive Communities: Connect with support groups or communities of parents who have experienced similar losses. These groups can offer true understanding and validation for your experiences and parenting choices.

Focus on Your Children's Needs: Remember that the primary goal is to address your children's emotional and developmental needs. Trust your instincts about what is best for them during this time.

Consult with Professionals: If unsure about your parenting approach, consider consulting with a grief coach, child psychologist, or family therapist. These professionals can provide guidance tailored to your family's specific situation.

Practice Self-Compassion: Be kind to yourself and recognize that parenting under the shadow of grief is challenging. Allow yourself the grace to make mistakes and learn as you go.

Reflect on Changes: Periodically reflect on the changes in your parenting style. Consider what is working and what might need adjustment, keeping the well-being of your family as the guiding principle.

Educate Others: Use your experience to educate others about grief and its impact on family dynamics. Sharing your story can be empowering and help build a more supportive environment around you.

Prioritize Family Bonding: Focus on activities that strengthen the bond within your family. This can effectively navigate through grief together and demonstrate to others the positive aspects of your evolving parenting style.

Remember, every family's journey through grief is unique, and there is no one-size-fits-all approach to parenting in such circumstances. Trust in your insight into your family's needs and your ability to adapt as a parent during this challenging time.

Parenting Children Through Grief

As we navigate the complexities of parenting in the aftermath of profound loss, it becomes crucial to not only manage our grief but also to support our children through theirs. In this section, we focus on practical and compassionate strategies you can employ to help your children cope with the loss of a sibling. These actionable tasks, drawn from expert research and grounded in real-world application, are designed to guide you in creating a nurturing and empathetic environment for your grieving family. Each task is a step towards healing, offering you and your children a path to navigate this challenging journey together.

Facilitate Open Communication: Encourage your children to express their feelings about the loss. Create a safe space where they can share their emotions without fear of judgment. Listen actively and validate their feelings.

Recognize Unique Grieving Styles: Understand that children may grieve differently than adults. Be attentive to changes in their behavior or mood, as these might be expressions of their grief.

Guide Them Through the Mourning Tasks: Help your children navigate J. William Worden's tasks of mourning. Assist them in accepting the loss, processing their grief, adjusting to life without the loved one, and finding enduring connections with the lost loved one.

Offer Age-Appropriate Explanations: Provide explanations about the loss that are appropriate for your children's age and developmental stage. Avoid euphemisms that confuse younger children, and be honest in a way they can comprehend.

Create Memory Rituals: Establish rituals or activities that help your children remember and honor the lost loved one. This can be as simple as lighting a candle, creating a memory box, or sharing stories about them.

Encourage Creative Expression: Support your children in expressing their grief through creative means like drawing, writing, or music. These activities can provide a therapeutic outlet for their emotions.

Maintain Routines: Try to keep daily routines as consistent as possible. Regular schedules can provide your children with a sense of stability and normalcy during this turbulent time.

Be a Model of Healthy Grieving: Show your children it's okay to grieve and express emotions. Your expression of grief can teach them healthy ways to cope with their feelings.

Seek Professional Support if Needed: If you notice signs of complicated grief in your children, such as persistent depressive symptoms or severe disruption in daily functioning, seek support from a mental health professional specializing in child bereavement.

Companioning Approach: Be a companion to your children in their grief journey. Walk alongside them, offering support and empathy rather than trying to direct or speed up their grieving process.

Remember, as a parent navigating your grief while supporting your children, self-care is also vital. Ensure you also seek the support and care you need during this time.

We hope that the insights and strategies shared here serve as a beacon of guidance and comfort. Navigating the journey of parenting in the midst of grief is a task that demands immense strength, patience, and compassion. The suggestions provided are intended to support you in this delicate balancing act, offering ways to manage your grief while also attending to the emotional and developmental needs of your children. We sincerely hope these insights provide practical assistance and reassure you that you are not alone on this journey. Remember, the path of parenting through grief is not only about guiding your children; it's also about allowing your family's love and resilience to shine through, even in the darkest of times. May this section offer support and hope for all parents facing the dual challenges of grieving and raising children.

CHAPTER 10

Navigating Social Currents and Keeping My Radar Clean in a World of Hurt

"Grief is like a long valley, a winding valley where any bend may reveal a totally new landscape."
—C. S. Lewis, A Grief Observed

As I, Kathy, reflect on the journey following Trevor's passing, I realize that one of my key strategies for coping was creating a personal sanctuary from the overwhelming external world. The constant barrage of news, societal struggles, and political turmoil felt too much for my strained emotional resources. My life needed my full attention, and trying to juggle the outside world's demands with my healing process was not feasible.

Navigating social events after experiencing such a profound loss felt akin to traversing a minefield. Simple inquiries like "How are you?", "Do you have kids?" and "How are the kids?" became loaded questions, each carrying a new, profound weight. In these moments, I learned to don a social mask, mastering the art of nodding and smiling while turmoil raged inside. Despite this inner conflict, there was a yearning to reconnect with the vibrancy of life, a longing for a sense of normalcy and reintegration into the community.

"Keeping my radar clean" became a vital strategy for self-preservation during this time. This meant consciously limiting my exposure to external stimuli that could exacerbate my emotional state. It involved creating boundaries around what I allowed into my mental and emotional space. I had to filter the information I consumed, the conversations I participated in, and the social situations I found myself in, not out of ignorance, but to protect my mental health and ensure I had the necessary space to heal.

This process of filtering and creating boundaries also extended to being mindful of the relationships and interactions that supported or hindered my healing process. It involved being honest about what I could handle and communicating my needs and limits to others, which sometimes meant declining social invitations, stepping back from certain friendships, or taking a break from news and social media. I understand that this approach might have seemed selfish or dismissive to some, and without the filter of my experience, it was likely hard for them to understand.

Ultimately, this approach was about respecting and honoring my limits. It was crucial in navigating the complex social currents in a world that often felt overwhelmingly full of hurt. By keeping my radar clean, I created a more manageable and nurturing environment, allowing healing to occur at a pace that suited my and my family's needs.

Here, I want to offer you permission to prioritize your own needs to choose what is best for your healing, even if others don't always understand it. This chapter explores the nuances of this approach, offering insights and strategies for those who find themselves needing to navigate their social landscapes amid personal grief. It's a journey through the delicate balance of safeguarding your fragile emotional state without severing the lifelines that social connections offer.

Her Quest for Enlightened Comprehension:

It was the first birthday party invitation since Trevor's passing. The card, adorned with cheerful balloons and bright colors, felt like a relic from a world that no longer existed for me. Holding the glossy paper between my fingers, I was acutely aware of the enormity of stepping back into a social setting brimming with small talk and laughter – especially one celebrating a child's growth, a poignant reminder of what we had lost.

Attending this party marked another significant realization of grief's impact on my life. It didn't go well. I managed about 30 minutes before the overwhelming sensation of the walls closing in on me took hold. Surrounded by happy faces and the sound of children's laughter, each child's visible growth stood in stark contrast to the halted progression of my son's life – a life that ended without reason or explanation. In desperation, I turned and ran, seeking refuge in deep breaths anywhere but in the midst of that celebration. I was ashamed of my inability to "rise above," and I silently vowed not to put myself in that position again.

From then on, we adopted an exit strategy for every event, or often, we declined invitations. It would be years before I could muster the courage to attend another child's birthday party. That change only came after proactive processing of grief and reconsolidation of the memories from that first scarring attempt. The experience left an indelible mark on my nervous system, a testament to the enduring power of grief.

His Path of Insightful Realization:

From the vantage point of a father who has endured the unimaginable loss of a child, my interactions with the world around me have fundamentally shifted. The conversations that once seemed routine, the everyday exchanges that make up the fabric of social life, now appear in a different light. I am less inclined to accept explanations or answers that lack depth or fail to acknowledge the complex nature of life and loss. I have a newfound skepticism, a questioning attitude that challenges superficial understandings and seeks deeper meaning in all things.

This shift in perspective also manifests in my tolerance for what I now perceive as "petty" issues. When engaging in conversations with other parents, I can't help but notice the contrast in our concerns. They worry about aspects of parenting and life that I used to dwell on, but now, after experiencing the profound loss of Trevor, these concerns seem trivial in comparison, such as their worries about academic performances, extracurricular activities, or minor behavioral issues pale in contrast to the irrevocable change that has shaped my existence.

This is not to diminish the validity of their experiences but to underscore how my perspective has changed. In the wake of profound grief, my definition of what constitutes a problem has shifted. I find myself impatient with conversations about "simpler" issues, not out of disrespect but because my experience of grief has redefined my priorities and perception of what truly matters in life.

Navigating these social dynamics is a challenge. It involves a careful balance between honoring my own journey and respecting the experiences of others. It means learning to engage with society and its diverse viewpoints while staying true to the profound lessons imparted by Trevor's loss. This chapter of life is about learning to coexist with a society that may not fully grasp the depths of child loss, yet is still seeking meaningful connections and empathy within it.

Research Perspectives:

In this section, we draw upon the insights of renowned experts in grief and bereavement to explore the intricate dynamics of social interactions following profound loss. We aim to offer support and understanding to those navigating the complexities of engaging socially while grappling with intense grief. This chapter not only delves into the emotional challenges faced in social settings but also provides suggestions on managing relationships with those around you. It emphasizes balancing honoring your grieving process and fostering open communication and education with others. Join us in uncovering ways to navigate these social currents with sensitivity and resilience.

Social Dynamics After Loss:

The work of Kenneth Doka and Terry Martin introduces the concept of "disenfranchised grief," which is particularly relevant in social situations for those who are grieving (Doka & Martin, 2010). This form of grief, often unrecognized or unsupported by society, can lead to feelings of isolation and a lack of empathy in social contexts.

Elisabeth Kübler-Ross, renowned for her groundbreaking work on the stages of grief, offers a framework for comprehending the internal emotional changes that affect external social interactions (Kübler-Ross, 1969). Her model illustrates how individuals in grief move through various emotional states, influencing their social involvement and tolerance for everyday issues. The stages of grief are not linear but represent a range of emotions that one might experience in any order and intensity during the grieving process, emphasizing the unique and personal ways people cope with loss.

Tolerance for Social Norms and Conversations:

Building upon Kübler-Ross's work, David Kessler explores how grief affects individuals' tolerance for social norms and the superficial aspects of interactions (Kessler, 2005). His insights shed light on the heightened sensitivity to what may seem trivial or inconsequential to those who have not experienced a similar loss.

Changes in Perception and Belief Systems:

George Bonanno's research into the varied trajectories of human resilience and grief elucidates how loss can lead to a profound shift in belief systems and perceptions, influencing social interactions (Bonanno, 2004). This shift can manifest in questioning previously held beliefs and a decreased tolerance for inauthentic or surface-level exchanges.

Strategies for Social Resilience:

M. Katherine Shear's studies on complicated grief suggest the importance of developing strategies for resilience in social settings, emphasizing the need for self-care and setting boundaries (Shear, 2015). Her work advocates finding a balance between engaging with others and honoring one's emotional needs.

Through this exploration of research perspectives, readers are offered a deeper understanding of the social challenges faced in the wake of child loss. They are provided with strategies to navigate these complexities with grace and self-compassion.

Enhancing Communication Post-Loss:

In addition to the insights of Doka, Martin, Kübler-Ross, Kessler, Bonanno, and Shear, it's crucial to consider the work of experts like Alan Wolfelt, known for his compassionate approach to grief counseling.

Wolfelt's emphasis on "companioning" rather than "treating" the bereaved underscores the importance of empathetic communication and the value of shared experiences in social interactions (Wolfelt, 2003). Here's an example of how empathetic communication might unfold in a conversation with someone grieving a loss:

Situation: You are talking to a friend who recently lost a loved one.

Non-Empathetic Communication:

"You must move on from this. It's been a while, and dwelling on it won't bring them back."

Empathetic Communication:

"I can see that you're hurting, and it's okay to feel this way. I'm here for you in any way you need, whether you want to talk about your feelings or just sit in silence. Your emotions are valid, and I want to understand your experience better. Can you tell me more about what you're going through?"

Maintaining and Managing Relationships:

Research by Therese Rando, a clinical psychologist specializing in grief therapy, provides valuable strategies for maintaining and managing relationships after a loss. Rando's work highlights the need for clear and honest communication with friends and family, advocating for expressing one's needs and setting boundaries to navigate social situations more effectively (Rando, 1988).

Educational Approaches in Social Settings:

Pauline Boss's concept of "ambiguous loss" is also relevant here, providing a framework for understanding the complexities of grief (Boss, 1999).

Boss's work can guide individuals in educating their social circles about the nature of their grief, fostering a deeper understanding among peers, leading to more supportive and accommodating interactions.

Navigating Loss: Suggestions & Support

In this chapter, we embark on a dual journey of insight and empathy. This journey is twofold: it delves into the world of the griever, exploring the self-support mechanisms crucial for navigating the personal labyrinth of loss, and it also opens a window into the lives of those around the griever, offering insights into how friends and family, and acquaintances can provide meaningful support.

From the griever's perspective, we explore strategies and tools that can aid in managing the overwhelming emotions and challenges accompanying loss. This includes practical steps for self-care, methods for processing grief, and ways to honor and maintain a connection with the lost loved one. The focus is on fostering resilience and finding a path toward healing that respects the individuality of each person's grief journey.

Simultaneously, we turn our attention to those who are in a position to offer support. Awareness of the complexities of grief is crucial for non-grievers to become effective allies. This section guides empathetic communication, appropriate ways to provide help, and insights into the do's and don'ts of supporting someone who is grieving. It's about building a bridge of compassion and empathy between the world of the griever and those who wish to support them.

Together, these perspectives weave a tapestry of support, offering a comprehensive guide for navigating the turbulent waters of loss. Whether you are in the midst of grief or standing beside someone who is, this section aims to equip you with the insight and tools necessary for this challenging yet deeply human experience.

Strategies for Navigating Social Waters While in Grief:

Setting Boundaries: It's okay to decide when and how you want to engage socially. Listen to your emotions and give yourself permission to decline invitations when you're not ready.

Preparing Responses: Think ahead about how to handle common questions or comments. Having a prepared response can reduce anxiety in social situations.

Seeking Understanding Companionship: Surround yourself with friends who understand your journey and are willing to provide the space and support you need.

Set Small, Achievable Goals: Focus on setting and accomplishing small tasks. This can help you regain a sense of control and accomplishment.

Honoring Your Grief in Social Settings: Find subtle ways to honor your grief, even in social settings. This could be a piece of jewelry that reminds you of your loved one or a quiet moment of reflection during the event.

Embracing Moments of Lightness: Allow yourself moments of joy and lightness without guilt. It's part of the healing process and doesn't diminish the love you have for the one you lost.

Communicating Your Needs: Don't hesitate to express your needs to close friends or hosts. People often want to help but may not know how.

Practicing Self-Care: After social interactions, take time for self-care. Whether it's a quiet evening at home or journaling, do what helps you recharge.

Navigating social currents after loss is about finding balance. It's about gradually reintegrating into the world around you while honoring the internal shifts grief has brought. This chapter is a guide to maneuvering these waters with grace and an ever-evolving sense of self.

Strategies for Supporting Others in Grief:

For friends, family, and acquaintances, interacting with someone who has experienced profound loss can be fraught with uncertainty. There's a fear of saying the wrong thing, of inadvertently causing pain. People often tread cautiously, sometimes too cautiously, leading to awkward conversations. The relationship dynamics evolve; what was once easy and light-hearted now requires a new level of sensitivity. A favorite quote of ours is, "If you simply cannot understand why someone is grieving so much for so long, consider yourself fortunate that you do not understand."

Listen Without Judgment: Offer an empathetic ear. Let the grieving person talk about their feelings or their loved one without feeling the need to offer solutions.

Acknowledge the Loss: Don't shy away from mentioning the lost loved one. Acknowledging the loss can be comforting.

Offer Practical Help: Provide specific offers of help, like running errands, cooking meals, or assisting with household tasks.

Be Patient: Understand that grief has no timeline. Be patient and offer your support for as long as it's needed.

Educate Yourself About Grief: Learn about the grieving process. Understanding what the grieving person might be going through can help you provide better support.

Check in Regularly: Keep in touch regularly, even if it's just a simple message to let them know you're thinking of them.

Respect Their Way of Grieving: Understand that everyone grieves differently. Respect their unique way of processing the loss. Your patience and support will go a long way in a very unsupportive society.

This dual approach – focusing on the individual experiencing loss and those around them – offers a holistic view of the grieving process. For the griever, we've explored various strategies and tools essential for managing overwhelming emotions and honoring the connection with the lost loved one. For friends, family, and acquaintances, we've provided guidance on becoming effective allies in this journey, emphasizing the importance of empathetic communication and practical support.

For further insight into how to support others in their grief, consider exploring Chapter 1, "Supporting Others in Grief: Empathetic Connection and Compassion," which offers clear guidelines on prioritizing support in the immediate aftermath of a loss. Additionally, Chapter 17, "Navigating Grief's Isolation and Relationship Changes," offers guidance on what to say and how to address shifts in social dynamics.

This section has explored the delicate art of balancing personal healing with social reintegration and the intricate dance of supporting others while respecting their unique grieving process. We hope the insights and strategies provided here will serve as a compassionate guide for those navigating their path through grief or standing beside someone who is. Remember, whether you're in the throes of loss or offering a shoulder to lean on, your journey is valid, and your efforts are a testament to the resilience of the human spirit and the power of empathy.

CHAPTER 11

Compassion Unleashed: Navigating Self-Compassion and Forgiveness for Others

"When we give ourselves compassion, we are opening our hearts in a way that can transform our lives."
—Kristin Neff

Our self-compassion exploded when we began to understand the physiological and psychological stress we were under. It became evident that our responses to grief were not just emotional reactions but also deeply rooted in our body's natural coping mechanisms. This realization brought a profound sense of relief and self-acceptance. We learned to appreciate the enormity of what we were experiencing and the incredible resilience it takes to navigate such a journey. In the depths of grief, we often become our own harshest critics. Thoughts like, "I could have done more" or "I should have been there" replay endlessly. Cultivating self-compassion means learning to silence these critical inner voices. It's about acknowledging that, while we did our best with the knowledge and resources we had, grief can still overwhelm the strongest of us. This chapter guides you through embracing kindness towards yourself, allowing for healing and acceptance in the wake of loss.

Forgiveness often extends beyond the self. It's also about recognizing with grace that those around us may not fully grasp the depths of our grief. They may offer well-intentioned but hurtful comments or seem impatient with the time it takes to heal. It takes awareness and skill to navigate these interactions with empathy and forgiveness, recognizing that everyone has limitations in understanding a level of grief they haven't experienced. One of our favorite books is *The Four Agreements* by Don Miguel Ruiz. In this book, Ruiz presents four personal freedom and self-development principles rooted in Toltec wisdom. The agreements are:

Be Impeccable with Your Word: Speak with integrity and say only what you mean. Avoid using words to speak against yourself or to gossip about others. Use the power of your word in the direction of truth and love.

Don't Take Anything Personally: Understand that nothing others do is because of you. What others say and do is a projection of their own reality, their own dreams.

Don't Make Assumptions: Find the courage to ask questions and to express what you really want. Communicate with others as clearly as you can to avoid misunderstandings, sadness, and drama.

Always Do Your Best: Your best is going to change from moment to moment; it will be different when you are healthy as opposed to sick. Under any circumstance, simply do your best, and you will avoid self-judgment, self-abuse, and regret (Ruiz, 1997).

These principles offer a framework for effective personal development and are valuable in fostering understanding, communication, and self-compassion. It is a transformative book that presents a simple yet effective code of personal conduct for leading a life of freedom, true happiness, and love. The two that stand out regarding this chapter are "Don't Take Anything Personally" and "Don't Make Assumptions."

In the context of navigating grief and interpersonal relationships: "Don't Take Anything Personally," Ruiz emphasizes that nothing others do is because of you but rather a projection of their reality, dreams, and wounds. When you internalize this agreement, you begin to see that the hurtful comments or actions of others are often not about you at all, but more often, it is about them! Embracing this principle means recognizing that their individual experiences and emotional states influence each person's response and behavior. By not taking things personally, you protect yourself from unnecessary suffering. This doesn't imply indifference or lack of empathy but rather a recognition that personal worth isn't dependent on external validation or reactions. It's about maintaining a sense of inner peace and self-worth, regardless of how others may behave or what they might say. In grief, where you are already handling profound emotional challenges, this agreement can be a powerful tool for maintaining emotional balance and fostering healing. It's liberating when you can choose not to get offended. (I would like to state that Peter was way better at this than I was initially. Many venting sessions later, I finally appreciated what he already knew.)

The agreement "Don't Make Assumptions" reminds those grieving to communicate openly and seek clarity in their interactions with others, thereby avoiding misunderstandings and additional emotional stress that can arise from unverified beliefs or expectations. This perspective is also liberating, especially when emotions run high, and interactions become fraught with misunderstandings. We urge you to seek clarity in interactions to avoid conflicts.

It's about balancing protecting our emotional well-being and extending grace to those who may inadvertently cause us pain as we navigate the complex terrain of human emotions and relationships.

Her Quest for Enlightened Comprehension:

That morning, as I stood in front of the mirror, the reflection looking back at me told a story deeper than the one I narrated to the world. It was a face etched with the lines of profound grief and the shadows of self-criticism and blame. Once windows to a soul filled with warmth, my eyes now carried a harshness, a piercing, critical gaze that bore into my very being. It was a moment of stark realization – the journey to self-compassion needed to begin, not tomorrow, but now, in this moment of painful self-awareness.

This journey was about silencing the inner critic and learning to view myself with the same empathy I would offer to a dear friend in my situation. It meant recognizing that the path of grief is fraught with complexities and that stumbling along this path did not equate to failure. I needed to embrace that healing is not linear, and self-forgiveness is integral to this process.

Simultaneously, this realization opened my eyes to the need to extend compassion towards others. I became more aware of the struggles hidden behind the facades people wear. I recognized that just as I was grappling with my inner demons, others, too, were fighting their silent battles. This fostered a sense of empathy for those around me, realizing that we are all navigating the turbulent waters of life's challenges, each in our unique way.

Embracing self-compassion meant learning to treat myself with kindness to allow myself moments of vulnerability without the weight of self-judgment. It was about learning to speak to myself with words of encouragement, acknowledging my pain, and honoring my journey.

In extending compassion to others, I practiced patience and offered grace more freely. I listened more intently, not just to respond but to understand. I learned to offer support not by imposing my perceptions but by being present and attuned to their needs.

The journey to self-compassion and extending compassion to others became intertwined paths. As I walked these paths, I found that they led to personal healing and deeper, more meaningful connections with those around me. It was a transformative process where cultivating kindness within became the foundation for spreading kindness to others.

His Path of Insightful Realization:

Before the loss of Trevor, my approach to interacting with parents who had experienced the unimaginable – the death of a child – was, in retrospect, marked by a lack of true understanding. My responses were shaped by discomfort and uncertainty, often resorting to clichéd expressions of sympathy or, worse, a well-intentioned but misguided attempt to steer conversations away from their pain. I realize now that my interactions, though well-meaning, fell short of providing the genuine support and empathy these grieving parents needed.

This stark realization came into focus after Trevor's passing when I found myself on the other side of the equation. In my journey of grief, I encountered responses from those around me that echoed my previous inadequacies. People often struggled to find the right words or chose to say nothing at all, leaving a chasm of unmet emotional needs. Their discomfort in addressing the depth of my loss was palpable, and through this, I gained a profound awareness of my past failures in supporting others in similar situations.

In this newfound clarity, I began to extend compassion and grace toward those who were at a loss when confronted with my grief. I saw reflections of my former self in their hesitations. I realized that their inability to provide the support I needed stemmed not from a lack of caring but from a lack of knowing how to navigate such profound sorrow. It fostered a sense of empathy within me for both my past self and for those around me who struggled to support me in my grief.

This experience has reshaped how I approach others in their times of loss. I've learned the importance of being present, listening more, and offering fewer platitudes. It's about acknowledging their pain, offering a shoulder to lean on, and simply being there, even in silence. This shift in perspective has aided in my healing process and equipped me to be a more effective source of comfort to others experiencing loss.

From this journey, I've realized the power of compassionate understanding and the necessity of being genuinely present for those grappling with grief. It's a lesson in humility and empathy, teaching me that sometimes, the best support we can offer is acknowledging that we don't have all the answers, but we are here to share in the journey, wherever it may lead.

Research Perspectives:

In this chapter, we explore the healing powers of self-compassion and the liberating journey of forgiveness in the context of grief. This chapter draws on the expertise of distinguished scholars and practitioners in the fields of psychology and grief. Their research offers practical strategies for those seeking to navigate the tumultuous waters of grief with kindness toward themselves and others.

This section is crafted to provide theoretical insights and offers tangible steps for integrating self-compassion and forgiveness into your healing journey. It is an invitation to embrace a gentle, forgiving approach to oneself and to navigate the complexities of interpersonal relationships affected by loss with empathy.

The Role of Self-Compassion in Grief:

Kristin Neff's research on self-compassion highlights its importance in coping with difficult emotions, including grief (Neff, 2003). Neff suggests that self-compassion involves being kind to oneself, recognizing that suffering is part of the shared human experience, and maintaining a balanced perspective on one's experiences.

Practicing Forgiveness:

The work of Robert Enright on forgiveness provides valuable insights into releasing self-blame and extending forgiveness to oneself and others (Enright, 2001). Enright emphasizes that forgiveness is a process that involves recognizing the pain, developing empathy, and making a conscious decision to forgive.

Balancing Grief and Self-Care:

M. Katherine Shear's studies on complicated grief shed light on the importance of self-compassion in the process of grieving and healing (Shear, 2015). Shear advocates for a balanced approach to grief that includes acknowledging one's pain and practicing self-care.

Navigating Forgiveness in Relationships:

David Kessler's exploration of grief and relationships touches on the complexity of forgiveness in the wake of loss, especially in forgiving oneself or others who may have inadvertently caused pain (Kessler, 2005).

By integrating these perspectives, readers are offered a comprehensive understanding of the importance of self-compassion and forgiveness in the grief process. These insights aim to empower individuals to navigate their grief with kindness towards themselves and others.

Navigating Loss: Suggestions & Support

Here, we offer practical and heartfelt strategies for cultivating these vital aspects of compassion. It acknowledges the difficulties faced in forgiving those who may have contributed to our pain, directly or indirectly. It guides readers in fostering a kind and forgiving attitude towards themselves during this vulnerable time.

Reflective Journaling: Write down your thoughts and feelings, particularly those of self-criticism or blame. Then, rewrite these thoughts from a compassionate standpoint.

Mindfulness and Meditation: Practice mindfulness to stay present and reduce self-judgment. Meditation can also be a tool for cultivating a more compassionate inner dialogue.

Seek Stories of Resilience: Read or listen to stories of others who have navigated grief. This can provide perspective and help you feel less alone in your journey.

Educate Your Circle: Gently educate friends and family about grief. This can foster patience in your social interactions.

Set Time Aside for Grief: Consider establishing support sessions as a space to work through feelings of self-blame and to develop strategies for self-compassion.

Practicing Gratitude: Focus on small moments of gratitude each day. This practice can shift your focus from loss to appreciation, aiding emotional healing.

Forgiveness Rituals: Engage in rituals that symbolize both self-forgiveness and forgiving others. This could be a symbolic act, like writing a letter of forgiveness and then burning it.

Self-Affirmation Exercises: Start your day with positive affirmations. Look in the mirror and affirm your strengths and your journey. Say things like, "I am doing my best," or "I am worthy of compassion and understanding."

Create a Self-Compassion Mantra: Develop a personal mantra that resonates with your journey towards self-compassion. Whenever you feel overwhelmed, repeat this mantra to yourself as a reminder of your commitment to treating yourself kindly.

Identify Triggers for Self-Criticism: Take note of situations or thoughts that trigger self-critical thoughts. Recognizing these triggers can help you prepare and respond with self-compassion rather than harsh judgment.

Practice Self-Forgiveness: Set aside time to reflect on any feelings of guilt or regret. Acknowledge these feelings without judgment and then consciously practice forgiving yourself, with an awareness that grief can cloud judgment and decision-making.

Connect with Supportive Others: Engage in conversations with friends or support groups who understand the journey of grief. Sharing your experiences with empathetic listeners can reinforce feelings of self-compassion and forgiveness.

Visualization Techniques: Use visualization to foster forgiveness and compassion. Imagine a scene where you offer kindness to yourself or visualize a peaceful interaction with someone you want to forgive.

Set Realistic Expectations for Yourself: Acknowledge that healing is a process and set realistic, compassionate goals for yourself. Celebrate small victories and progress in your journey of self-compassion and forgiveness.

Attend Workshops or Seminars: Participate in workshops or seminars on self-compassion and forgiveness. Learning new perspectives and techniques can enhance your ability to integrate these practices into your life.

The paths of self-kindness and forgiveness are deeply personal and can vary greatly from one individual to another. The strategies and insights offered in this section are intended to be a gentle guide, helping you to navigate these paths with greater ease. By embracing self-compassion, you allow yourself the space and grace to heal, and through forgiveness, you open the door to newfound peace and liberation. May these suggestions empower and support you as you navigate the complex yet rewarding journey of healing and growth through compassion and forgiveness.

CHAPTER 12

Navigating Anger, Guilt, and Regret in Grief's Dance

"The bitterest tears shed over graves are for words left unsaid and deeds left undone." —Harriet Beecher Stowe

We noticed that we were often right on the cusp of feeling irritated or even angry. At first, we thought it was part of becoming "that stranger" we discussed in an earlier chapter, a version of ourselves unfamiliar and altered by grief. However, as we delved deeper into our emotions, we realized that these feelings of anger, guilt, and regret were integral components of our grieving process. They were not anomalies but rather natural responses to the profound loss we had experienced. In this chapter, we explore these intense and often uncomfortable emotions accompanying the journey of grief. Anger is grief's best friend. Grief and anger often emerge as powerful, perplexing companions. It can manifest in unexpected outbursts or simmer quietly under the surface. Anger in grief is complex; it's a reaction to the unfairness of loss, a protest against a reality that has been irrevocably altered. Navigating anger and recognizing it as a natural part of the grieving process opens the door to exploring it and finding ways to express it constructively.

Guilt and regret are the uninvited guests in grief's journey. They lurk in the corners of our minds, raising questions like, "Could I have done something different?" or "Why didn't I see the signs?" These emotions are insidious, as they can trap us in a cycle of self-blame and what-ifs. This chapter focuses on acknowledging these feelings, understanding their roots, and learning to release their hold on us. It's about transforming guilt and regret into lessons of compassion and acceptance.

This chapter seeks to unravel the complexities of these feelings, understand their roots, and learn how to navigate them with compassion and awareness. We address the challenges of dealing with anger that can arise unexpectedly, the guilt that often follows thoughts of what could have been done differently, and the regret that lingers over unsaid words or actions not taken. This part of our journey is not just about recognizing these emotions but also about finding ways to heal and grow from them. It's a crucial step in transforming our grief into a dance of healing, where every step guides us toward acceptance and peace, no matter how painful.

Her Quest for Enlightened Comprehension:

In those early days, I half-expected my heart to cease or wished for a swift, collective end for my family – a miracle that remained elusive. My anger towards God became a constant companion during those months. It was anger born from confusion, from the deep-seated belief that we, as parents, must have missed some crucial sign in Trevor or that he could have shifted something so that this could have played out differently. The questions of "why" and "how" spiraled endlessly in my mind, each unanswered query fueling my resentment. I felt abandoned by a faith that I had once leaned on, now questioning its very foundations in the wake of our loss.

Equally tumultuous was my anger towards others. I was infuriated by their inability to grasp the extent of my heartache, their well-meaning but often misguided attempts to dictate where I should be in my grief journey. It seemed as though everyone had an opinion on how I should handle my sorrow, yet none could fathom the depth of the abyss into which I had fallen.

I existed in a state where time and emotions were in constant flux, often stuck in a moment while the world relentlessly moved forward. People around me expected progression, a steady march toward healing, but grief does not adhere to timelines or expectations. I was where I was, angry – in a place of raw, unfiltered mourning that refused to be boxed into stages or timeframes. I used to joke that anger was higher than grief on the emotional scale, and therefore, being angry was preferred over grief.

This journey through grief was a solitary path, punctuated by moments of loneliness and misunderstanding. Yet, it was also a path that led to profound self-discovery. I learned to embrace my emotions in all their complexity, to allow myself the grace to be angry, to question, and to mourn in my way, on my terms. This process of internal reckoning was not just about coming to terms with Trevor's loss; it was also about redefining my relationship with myself, with my faith, and with those around me.

His Path of Insightful Realization:

In the raw aftermath of losing Trevor, I felt the stirrings of anger bubbling beneath the surface of my grief. It was a seething, restless emotion, ready to erupt at the slightest provocation. But I made a conscious decision – I would not let this anger take root in me, to consume and define my grief. Instead, I chose to acknowledge it and then actively work to release it, to purge it from my system before it had the chance to overshadow the love and memories I held for my son.

My approach to dealing with this anger was multifaceted. Firstly, I recognized it as a natural response to the profound injustice of losing a child. It was okay to feel angry; it was a valid part of my grief. But I also knew that unchecked, it could spiral into bitterness and resentment, emotions that would hinder my ability to heal and find peace.

I turned to physical outlets to channel this anger. At the time, we had a wood stove, so chopping wood, tossing chopped wood into a pile, and hauling chopped wood into the house were great ways to release anger safely. Numerous projects around the house required swinging a hammer. And hey, those had a great outcome of improving our home as well.

This journey of managing anger was not about suppressing it or pretending it didn't exist. It was about facing it head-on, giving it space, and then consciously working to let it go. It was a vital part of my grieving process – a way to ensure that my memories of Trevor were not tainted by unbridled rage but were instead a reflection of the love, however, tinged with sadness that will always define his place in my heart.

Research Perspectives:

Anger is a complex and often misunderstood emotion in the context of grief. Anger can manifest in myriad ways during the grieving process, serving as both a natural response to loss and a barrier to healing if not acknowledged and addressed. Drawing upon the expertise of renowned psychologists and grief specialists, we explore the multifaceted nature of anger in grief. This exploration aims to provide a deeper comprehension of how anger can emerge as a part of grief, its various expressions, and the importance of integrating this emotion into the healing journey. By examining these insights, we seek to offer a comprehensive perspective on anger's role in grief, providing support and guidance for those navigating this challenging aspect of their journey.

Anger in Grief:

The work of George Bonanno sheds light on the diverse trajectories of grief, including the role of anger as a common, yet often misunderstood, response to loss (Bonanno, 2004). Bonanno's research helps us understand that, while potentially disruptive, anger can also be a part of the natural grieving process, serving as an emotional outlet for the bereaved.

Exploring the Manifestation of Anger in Grief:

Research by Colin Murray Parkes, a prominent figure in the study of bereavement, emphasizes that anger in grief can often be directed toward oneself, others, or even abstract entities like fate or God (Parkes, 1972). Parkes' work helps us understand that this anger is a normal response to the sense of injustice and powerlessness felt in grief.

The Role of Anger in the Mourning Process:

J. William Worden, known for his Four Tasks of Mourning, identifies that experiencing and expressing anger is a critical part of coming to terms with the reality of the loss (Worden, 2009). Worden's model suggests that working through this anger is essential for healing.

Anger as a Component of Grieving Styles:

Kenneth Doka and Terry Martin's concept of "grieving styles" includes the expression of anger as a valid and individual response to loss (Doka

& Martin, 2010). They highlight that how one experiences and expresses anger can vary greatly and is influenced by personal coping styles and cultural norms.

Physiological Aspects of Anger in Grief:

Bessel van der Kolk's research into the body's response to trauma and loss indicates that anger can also have a physiological dimension, often stemming from the fight-or-flight response activated by grief (van der Kolk, 2014). This perspective offers that anger is a natural bodily response to the trauma of loss.

Exploring the Origins of Guilt and Regret in Grief: Research indicates guilt and regret often stem from feelings of unfinished business or perceived shortcomings in one's relationship with the loved one (Johnson & Smith, 2021). Awareness of the source of these feelings can be the first step in addressing them.

Research on ACT and Grief:

According to Hayes and Smith, Acceptance and Commitment Therapy is effective in helping individuals process grief by encouraging acceptance of their emotional experiences and commitment to a meaningful life despite the loss (Hayes & Smith, 2022). This approach helps in reducing the intensity of grief-related stress and enhances psychological flexibility.

Processing Guilt and Regret:

Therese Rando's extensive research on bereavement and coping mechanisms highlights the prevalence of guilt and regret in grief (Rando, 1993). Her insights reveal how these feelings can stem from thoughts of perceived inadequacy in preventing the loss or from things left unsaid or undone.

The Role of Self-Forgiveness in Healing:

Self-forgiveness is crucial to healing from guilt and regret. Research by Thompson et al. (2019) highlights the therapeutic value of self-forgiveness in the grieving process, noting its role in reducing emotional distress and facilitating acceptance.

The Journey Towards Forgiveness and Acceptance:

Robert Enright's pioneering work in the study of forgiveness provides a framework for how forgiveness, both of oneself and others, can play a crucial role in healing from grief (Enright, 2001). Enright's approach emphasizes the importance of acknowledging and processing these emotions as steps toward emotional reconciliation.

Strategies for Managing Complex Grief Emotions:

M. Katherine Shear's studies offer strategies for managing complicated grief, including the complex emotions of anger, guilt, and regret (Shear, 2015). She advocates for a therapeutic approach that involves recognizing these emotions and their roots and learning to integrate them into the grieving process.

By exploring these research perspectives, this chapter aims to understand better how anger, guilt, and regret intertwine within the grieving process. It offers insights and tools for navigating these emotions, fostering a journey toward informed and compassionate healing.

Navigating Loss: Suggestions & Support

Managing intense feelings is essential for navigating the complex terrain of grief. Anger in grief can be perplexing and overwhelming, manifesting in various forms and intensities. Through the guidance offered here, you are invited to explore practical strategies to acknowledge, express, and regulate this powerful emotion. The aim is to provide you with tools and insights that empower you to handle anger in a healthy and conducive way to your healing process. As you read through these actionable tasks, remember that experiencing anger during grief is not only common but also a natural part of the emotional landscape of loss. This section is designed to help you navigate this aspect of grief with compassion and practical steps toward emotional balance.

Acknowledge and Express Anger Safely: Recognize and accept that feeling angry is a natural part of grieving. It's okay to feel anger – don't push it away or judge yourself for experiencing it. Find safe ways to express your anger through physical activity, creative expression, talking it out with a trusted friend or professional, or even shouting into a pillow.

Reflect on the Source of Your Anger: Spend time reflecting on what triggers your anger. Is it rooted in feelings of helplessness, injustice, or something else? Becoming aware of the source can help in managing it better.

Journal About Your Anger: Write down instances when you feel angry, what triggered it, and how you responded. Journaling can help you track patterns and progress in dealing with your anger.

Practice Relaxation Techniques: Engage in deep breathing, meditation, or yoga. These can help calm your mind and body, making it easier to handle anger when it arises.

Develop a Routine for Difficult Days: When anger seems overwhelming, have a plan. This might include activities that soothe you, such as engaging in a hobby or listening to a specific playlist of music, people you can talk to, or safe spaces where you can be alone.

Challenge Negative Thought Patterns: When spiraling into negative thoughts that fuel your anger, try to challenge and reframe them. Remind yourself of the context and seek a more balanced perspective.

Create a Physical Outlet: Engage in regular physical activity, like running, swimming, or boxing, which can be an outlet for pent-up anger and frustration.

Explore Anger Management Techniques: Consider learning specific anger management strategies, such as cognitive-behavioral techniques, which can help identify and alter patterns of angry reactions.

Cognitive-Behavioral Techniques for Managing Guilt: Cognitive-behavioral therapy (CBT) offers valuable tools for reframing negative thoughts that contribute to feelings of guilt and regret. Techniques such as journaling and cognitive restructuring can help individuals reevaluate and shift their perspective on past events.

Practicing Mindfulness: Mindfulness helps acknowledge and accept your thoughts and feelings about loss without judgment. Simple practices like mindful breathing or mindful walking can be beneficial.

Identifying Personal Values: Engage in exercises to clarify your values. Acceptance and Commitment Therapy (ACT) emphasizes living a life consistent with your values, even in the face of grief. Reflect on what is most important to you and how you can continue to live, aligning with these values. Then, commit to value-driven actions: Once you identify your values, commit to taking actions that align with them. This could involve activities that connect you to others, honor your loved one, or engage in hobbies or causes that are meaningful to you.

Reflect on the Source of Guilt: Take time to understand where your guilt is coming from. Reflect on whether these feelings are based on realistic self-assessment or are magnified by your grief.

Challenge Regret with Reality: Counteract regret by reminding yourself of the realities and limitations of what you knew and could do at the time.

Seek Stories of Similar Experiences: Hearing about how others have navigated these emotions can provide perspective and lessen feelings of isolation.

Create Rituals for Release: Engage in personal rituals that symbolize the release of anger, guilt, and regret, such as writing letters to your lost loved one and then burning them.

Practice Self-Forgiveness: Work on forgiving yourself as part of the healing process. Remember that grief can cloud judgment and enhance self-criticism.

In embracing these strategies, you pave the way for a journey of healing that acknowledges and transforms anger into a stepping stone toward profound personal growth.

CHAPTER 13

Rediscovering Joy: Whatever Makes Your Heart Beat Again

"Find out where joy resides, and give it a voice far beyond singing. For to miss the joy is to miss all."
—Robert Louis Stevenson

Shortly after Trevor passed, we noticed that seeing cardinals fly gave us a sense that Trevor was near, signaling a small but poignant reminder of his presence. This observation expanded into a broader interest in bird watching, and soon, spending time outdoors became critically important to us. The simple sight of birds and the sound of music became our sanctuary – these elements were distracting or mysterious enough to capture our attention. But either way, it was in these moments, amidst birds and music, that we felt closest to Trevor. This newfound connection to nature and melody seemed to bridge the gap between our world and his, offering a sense of closeness that was both comforting and healing.

From the griever's perspective, the quest for joy can feel like chasing a mirage. The world often seems void of color, and activities that once brought happiness may now seem hollow or distant. Here, we will explore the notion that joy, although elusive, is not gone. It's about gently testing the waters of activities that once brought happiness or discovering new ones that speak to your evolving self. For us, the birds and music unexpectedly became a source of solace and connection. It's a journey of acknowledging that joy does not negate your loss but exists alongside it, a testament to your capacity for resilience and growth.

From the supporter's perspective, facilitating joy can be complex. It's about offering support without pressure, recognizing that their path back to joy is personal and cannot be rushed. This chapter focuses on being an ally in their search for joy – by being present, listening, and perhaps gently encouraging, but always respecting their pace and emotional space. Whether through nature, music, or any other means, the journey back to joy is deeply personal and reflective of each individual's unique connection to their lost loved one.

Her Quest for Enlightened Comprehension:

I recall vividly the moment when a flicker of joy first tried to penetrate the dense fog of my grief. Much like any other since we lost Trevor, it was an ordinary day cloaked in the somber hues of sorrow. But then, something unexpected happened. There was laughter – a genuine, spontaneous burst from something funny the kids did. For a split second, I found myself caught up in the moment, a smile breaking through the barriers I had unconsciously erected around my heart.

The sensation, however, was fleeting and left me disoriented. It felt like an intruder, an emotion out of place in the landscape of my mourning. The laughter echoed in my ears, starkly contrasting the silence that grief had brought into my life. I felt a pang of guilt almost immediately, as if that brief moment of lightness was a betrayal of Trevor's memory. How could I find space for joy when my world had been so irrevocably altered?

Yet, as I sat with these conflicting feelings, I realized this. This moment of lightness did not diminish the depth of my love or the pain of my loss. Instead, it was a sign that life still held moments of beauty and laughter, even if they were fleeting. It was a reminder that grief and joy could coexist, each emotion lending depth to the other, but that I had to allow it and know that it was okay to feel discomfort as I learned this new skill! Embracing this duality became a delicate endeavor. I learned to let these moments of joy, however slight or brief, be without the accompanying weight of guilt. I found joy in simple things: the warmth of the sun on my face, the comforting aroma of coffee in the morning, the sight of a blooming flower, or, my favorite, the sound of a bird I wasn't familiar with. These instances didn't erase my grief but offered a respite, a gentle reminder that the world still held wonder.

Rediscovering joy also meant re-engaging with life. I started seeking activities that once brought happiness—getting outside, where Trevor loved to be, where we had spent many joyful hours. At first, it was bittersweet, but over time, being outside became therapeutic, a connection to the cycle of life and growth, a basic need I had to have.

I also learned to listen and share more with those around me, discovering that joy often resides in connection and shared experiences. Each shared story and moment of empathy or laughter with friends and family became a step towards reclaiming the happiness that grief had overshadowed.

Rediscovering joy amidst grief was not a betrayal of my loss; it was an homage to the love that will always linger. It was an acknowledgment that even in the darkest times, the human spirit can find light and moments of joy to soothe the aching heart.

His Path of Insightful Realization:

For as long as I can remember, helping others has been a source of profound joy for me. There's a unique satisfaction and fulfillment that comes from being of service, from knowing that, in some small way, I am making a difference in someone else's life. After Trevor's passing, this aspect of my personality became a beacon of light, guiding me through the darker days of grief. In these moments of reaching out and offering support to others, I found a sense of purpose, a reminder that even amidst sorrow, I could contribute to the world positively.

My hands found solace in the act of creation and repair, in the tangible results of working on projects and making home repairs. These activities became more than just tasks; they were a form of therapy. The focus and concentration required for these projects provided a respite from the endless cycle of grief-related thoughts. Each completed task was a small victory, a step towards reclaiming a sense of normalcy and accomplishment.

But beyond all, the truest source of joy for me has always been rooted in my family – in the happiness of my kids and spouse. In the wake of our loss, spending time together as a family took on a new level of significance. We created new memories, realizing that while we carry the pain of our loss, we also carry the love and the legacy of Trevor with us. Simple yet profound moments, from shared meals to family outings, became cherished experiences, filling the void with laughter and love.

Listening to my children talk about their interests, dreams, and even mundane daily experiences became a source of delight. In their narratives, I found an escape from my grief and a window into their resilient spirits. Their enthusiasm and perspectives on life reminded me of life's endless possibilities and joys.

Rediscovering joy in these ways wasn't about moving on from our loss but moving forward with it. It was about finding ways to integrate the joy of the present with the love and memories of the past. Each act of helping others, each project completed, and every moment spent with my family became part of a larger tapestry of healing and rediscovery. They were reminders that even in the depths of sorrow, life's capacity for joy persists, waiting to be embraced in whatever form it may take.

Research Perspectives:

Here, we embark on a journey of reawakening to life's pleasures in the wake of profound grief. We draw upon the insights of renowned grief experts to guide and support those navigating the challenging but essential process of rediscovering joy and purpose. This section delves into the psychological underpinnings of joy in the context of grief, exploring how positive emotions can coexist with sorrow and their role in the healing process, and how to gently re-embrace the aspects of life that bring happiness and fulfillment, even in the midst of grief.

The Psychological Process of Rediscovering Joy:

Colin Murray Parkes' work on the psychosocial transitions in grief highlights the gradual process of re-engaging with life and finding joy after loss (Parkes, 1972). Parkes suggests that rediscovering joy is a significant part of adapting to loss, helping individuals to integrate the experience into their lives.

The Role of Positive Emotions in Grief:

Barbara Fredrickson's research on positive emotions, including joy, emphasizes their role in building resilience and coping with life's challenges (Fredrickson, 2001). Her Broaden-and-Build theory explains how positive emotions can expand one's perspective and foster personal growth, even in grief. It is also essential to recognize that experiencing joy does not diminish grief and can be a healthy part of the healing process.

Engaging in Meaningful Activities:

M. Katherine Shear's studies on complicated grief underscore the importance of engaging in meaningful activities that bring a sense of joy and purpose (Shear, 2015). Shear advocates for the therapeutic value of reconnecting with interests and passions as a pathway to healing.

Social Connections and Joy:

George Bonanno's research on resilience in grief highlights the significance of maintaining social connections and engaging in social activities to experience moments of joy and laughter (Bonanno, 2004). He emphasizes that social support is crucial in the healing process.

The journey to joy after loss is as unique as the individual experiencing it. We hope these insights help construct a valuable roadmap for this journey, highlighting the transformative power of positive emotions and the importance of re-engaging with life. Remember, rediscovering joy does not mean leaving behind the memory of your loved one; instead, it is about finding a balance where grief and joy can coexist, each lending depth to the other. As you move forward, hold onto the knowledge that it is possible to find moments of happiness and meaning amidst grief, and these moments can be a testament to your resilience and capacity for growth.

Navigating Loss: Suggestions & Support

The path to rediscovering joy is not about forgetting your loss but finding ways to let light back into your heart. We encourage you to embrace life's pleasures, big and small, as you continue to honor your grief journey. Embrace these strategies with an open heart and mind, allowing them to lead you toward moments of happiness and a renewed sense of purpose.

Explore Old and New Interests: Revisit hobbies or activities you once loved or explore new ones that spark your curiosity. This can be a powerful way to reconnect with yourself.

Create Small Moments of Pleasure: Focus on small, everyday joys – the warmth of the sun, a favorite song, a walk in nature. These moments can gradually reintroduce joy into your life.

Connect with Others: Share time with people who understand and respect your journey and pace. Supporters should be patient and avoid pushing the bereaved towards joy or closure before they are ready. Sometimes, joy can be reignited in the company of others.

Reflect on Your Journey: Journal or meditate on your experiences. Reflecting on how far you've come can be a source of inner joy and strength.

Be Open to New Experiences: Allow yourself to be open to new experiences, even if they feel daunting at first. New experiences can bring unexpected joy.

Cultivate a Gratitude Practice: Start each day by listing things you are grateful for. This practice can shift your focus toward positive aspects of life, fostering a sense of joy and appreciation.

Engage in Creative Expression: Whether it's painting, writing, music, or any other form of creative expression, immerse yourself in activities that allow you to express and process your emotions creatively.

Seek Out Laughter: Watch a comedy, listen to a funny podcast, or spend time with friends who make you laugh. Laughter can be a powerful tool for lifting spirits and finding moments of joy.

Volunteer or Help Others: Helping others can provide a sense of purpose and joy. Volunteer for a cause you care about or offer to help someone in need.

Plan Something to Look Forward To: Organize a small event or activity in the future. Having something to look forward to can bring a sense of hope and excitement.

Spend Time in Nature: Nature has a calming and rejuvenating effect. Spend time outdoors, whether walking in the park, hiking, or just sitting in a garden.

Celebrate Small Achievements: Acknowledge and celebrate your small victories and steps forward in your grief journey. Recognizing your progress can bring a sense of accomplishment and joy.

Join a Group or Club: Consider joining a group or club that aligns with your interests. This can be a great way to meet like-minded people and engage in activities that bring joy.

Practice Mindfulness: Engage in mindfulness exercises to stay present in the moment. This can enhance your appreciation of the small joys in everyday life.

Rediscover Music: Music can be incredibly therapeutic. Listen to your favorite songs, explore new genres, or even learn to play an instrument.

Rediscovering joy after a significant loss is not about forgetting your grief but about finding a way to live with it, allowing moments of happiness to seep back into your life. It's a journey of the heart, seeking and embracing whatever makes it beat with hope and joy. Remember that the journey to rediscovering joy is deeply personal and unique to each individual. Hold onto the belief that joy and grief can coexist, and allow yourself to experience moments of happiness without guilt. As you navigate this journey, be patient with yourself, knowing that each small step towards joy is a testament to your resilience and capacity for growth in the face of life's greatest challenges.

CHAPTER 14

Navigating the Calendar: Holidays, Anniversaries, Birthdays

"Grief is the last act of love we have to give to those we loved.
Where there is deep grief, there was great love."
—Unknown

It's important to note that one of the most profound lessons in our journey was that long before our brain recognized a holiday or special date was approaching, our hearts and hurting souls were already feeling the weight of it. This prelude of sorrow would be fascinating if it weren't so deeply affecting. Our emotions would start to stir and intensify weeks before the event, leading to prolonged periods of distress. However, after a few years, we noticed that, in most cases, the anticipation of the event was harder to bear than the day itself. This realization became a cornerstone of our coping strategy: keeping our focus on getting through these periods intact. Knowing that the heightened feelings were temporary made them more bearable, making the experience more manageable.

For grievers, navigating significant dates like holidays, anniversaries, and birthdays after a loss is indeed a complex dance of emotions. Once markers of joy and celebration, these occasions can transform into periods of intensified grief. This chapter guides you through finding ways to honor the memory of your loved one while managing the bittersweet emotions these days bring. It's about creating a balance between remembrance and moving forward, realizing that it's okay to feel joy amidst sorrow and that honoring their memory can coexist with creating new traditions.

Supporters of those who are grieving often face challenges in how to offer support, especially during significant dates like holidays, anniversaries, and birthdays. It requires a delicate balance of acknowledging the loss, offering help, respecting the individual's choices on how they wish to spend these days, and, importantly, maintaining flexibility. A key concern for someone in grief is the fear of feeling obligated to participate in events when their emotional reserves are depleted.

In this context, the "Spoon Theory" offers a valuable metaphor to explain the fluctuating energy levels of someone in grief. Originally created by Christine Miserandino to describe energy management for those with chronic illness, this theory equally applies to grief. Each task a person performs throughout the day, including participating in social events or even simple activities like getting dressed, consumes a certain amount of energy, represented as "spoons." Everyone has a limited number of spoons each day, and once they are used up, rest is needed to regain energy. This necessitates careful planning and prioritization of tasks to conserve energy.

The Spoon Theory helps us understand the need to manage and conserve energy, bringing awareness to the physical and emotional limitations experienced during grief. It's particularly helpful for supporters, as it explains why someone who is grieving might need to rest more or opt out of certain activities. Their available "spoons" or energy reserves might be limited, making it essential for them to choose how they expend their energy wisely.

As this chapter focuses on the perspectives of grievers and their supporters, it aims to provide insights and guidance for navigating the calendar of grief – a journey marked by remembrance, resilience, and that managing one's energy is a crucial part of the grieving process. It underscores the importance of empathy, flexibility, and recognizing the individual's right to manage their energy in a way that best supports their healing journey.

Her Quest for Enlightened Comprehension:

As the first day of school approaches, a familiar, poignant ache settles in my heart each year. It's a day marked by a flurry of activity, captured in cheerful photographs of children in their new outfits, with bright backpacks and beaming smiles. But for me, it's a stark reminder of what's missing. The sight of these images, so full of life and anticipation, brings a wave of sorrow for the milestones we'll never see with Trevor.

The first day of school, once a time of joyful chaos and excited chatter in our home, now feels like navigating a field of emotional landmines. I see other children posing on their doorsteps, and I can't help but envision Trevor among them. What would he have worn? What new adventures would he have been excited about? These questions linger, unanswered, in the air.

Social media becomes a mosaic of what could have been – each photo a glimpse into a world that feels intimately familiar and painfully out of reach. I find myself scrolling through a mix of happiness for these children and a deep, hollow sadness for my own. The dichotomy of these emotions is jarring, a testament to the complex layers of grief.

This day each year forces me to confront the permanence of our loss anew. While life moves forward for others, our family's narrative has been irrevocably altered. It's a day when Trevor's absence feels more pronounced and acute. I'm reminded not just of the loss of his presence but of the experiences and memories we won't get to share. It is one of those secondary losses that hit yearly, as Trevor should proceed through school.

Yet, amidst this pain, a subtle strength also emerges. I reach out to connect with others who understand, seeking comfort in shared experiences. I've learned to create small rituals to honor Trevor on this day – perhaps lighting a candle or looking through old photos, allowing myself a moment to reflect and remember.

Pictures from the first day of school will forever remind us of what we've lost, reminders of the milestones Trevor will never experience. In the midst of sorrow, there's a bittersweet gratitude for the time we had, the memories that we will always cherish, and the love and joy that Trevor brought to our lives.

Trevor passed in August, so from this point to January, it has felt like an unrelenting assault by the calendar: each month, another holiday, another hit. A sequence of dates that once held anticipation and joy but now are tinged with sorrow and longing. One after another, each a poignant reminder of our family's loss. The festive lights and decorations that adorn the streets mock the darkness within me. Halloween, Thanksgiving, Christmas – these celebrations, once the highlight of our family's year, now feel like hurdles to overcome. Each holiday is a stark reminder of the empty chair at the table, the unopened gifts, and the absence of Trevor's laughter mingling with the festive cheer.

By the time January arrives, the cumulative effect of these months leaves me feeling like a wrecked, wrangled mess. The joy and togetherness that these occasions are supposed to represent feel overshadowed by grief, exhaustion, and never-ending conflict from those who do not understand this journey. It's a time when the world celebrates new beginnings and resolutions, but for me, it's a period of reflecting on what's been irrevocably lost while trying to regroup, recharge, and try again this year.

The weight of grief is not just in the aching absence of Trevor; it's also entangled with the emotional strain of meeting social expectations and others' perceptions of how I should grieve. I realized early on that the exertion of maintaining a facade of strength and engaging in traditions when my heart was in rebellion was exhausting and counterproductive. It felt like a charade that left me more depleted. With our extended family unable to provide the support we needed, we, as a nuclear family, found ourselves navigating these poignant holidays in solitude. We began to forge new traditions that could bring us moments of joy without the poignant reminder of the empty chair symbolizing Trevor's absence. These new practices became our way of celebrating while still honoring the space where Trevor once was, a balance of remembering and living.

In this relentless cycle of grief, I also find moments of resilience. Each time I make it through these days, I am reminded of my strength and the enduring love that carries me through. I am reminded of my husband and me discussing how to navigate this as a family unit best. These moments don't erase the pain, but they provide a glimmer of hope – a reminder that even in the depths of sorrow, I can endure and find small ways to honor Trevor's memory.

The "assault of the calendar" is a testament to the enduring nature of grief – it doesn't ebb with time but changes, presenting new challenges and moments of reflection. As I brace myself each year for this cycle, I learn to navigate these days with a mixture of sorrow and resilience, honoring my grief while also acknowledging my capacity to withstand and persevere.

His Path of Insightful Realization:

The Christmas tree stood solemnly in the corner of the living room, its lights twinkling softly, casting a gentle glow in the otherwise dim space. Our first Christmas without Trevor brought a more profound void than I imagined. There was only silence where there should have been the sound of his laughter and the rustle of him rummaging through gifts.

I remember feeling as though I was caught in an emotional tug-of-war. Part of me wanted to uphold the holiday traditions for our other children, to give them a sense of normalcy and joy they deserved. Yet, another part of me wanted to surrender to the grief, to let the day slip by unnoticed, as if marking it would somehow deepen the pain of his absence. Those initial holidays were an excruciating blend of sorrow and forced festivity. Others imposed rigid expectations of how we should navigate the holiday, often leading to conflict due to their forceful approach. The absence of support during those initial years of grief has become a lasting reminder of the importance of setting boundaries and prioritizing our emotional well-being; this challenging time highlighted the necessity of self-advocacy and the pursuit of a healing journey that is personal and unique rather than one dictated by the expectations of others. This experience was a powerful lesson in the importance of following our path to healing, regardless of how it may differ from what others believe is best for us.

The truth is, even as time passes, holidays still carry a weight of loss, a reminder of the space that used to be filled by Trevor. During holidays, the contrast between our grieving family and the celebratory world can be strikingly pronounced, often deepening our sense of isolation. In these moments, our grief becomes especially stark against widespread seasonal cheer, making us feel unsupported and disconnected.

As we navigated these holidays, we learned to balance honoring Trevor's memory and creating new ways to experience joy. We started new traditions, including moments to remember him, like lighting a candle, sharing stories about him, spreading his ashes, or finding a new ornament for his Trevor Tree that stays up year-round. These acts became a crucial part of our holiday rituals, a way to keep his spirit alive in our celebrations. The journey through the holidays as a grieving family is ongoing, each year bringing challenges and reflections. We've learned to lean on each other, to find comfort in our shared memories of Trevor. While the holidays will always be tinged with sadness, they have also become a time to celebrate his life, to remember the joy he brought us, and to acknowledge how he shaped our family in ways that continue to resonate, even in his absence.

Research Perspectives:

This section addresses the sensitive and challenging experience of facing significant dates, holidays, and milestones while navigating the grief journey. By presenting the insights of experts in grief and bereavement, we aim to provide empathy for those contending with the complexities of such occasions. Our goal is to offer a compassionate perspective on how holidays, anniversaries, and birthdays can influence the grieving process, equipping you with advice for coping and honoring these significant milestones in a way that respects your unique journey through grief.

Coping with Milestones in Grief:

Colin Murray Parkes' research on grief emphasizes the significance of anniversaries and special dates in the grieving process (Parkes, 1972). He notes that these dates often reignite the pain of loss and can be times of heightened emotional distress, but also opportunities for remembrance and honoring the lost loved one.

The Role of Rituals in Grief:

Therese Rando has extensively explored how rituals and commemorative activities can aid in grieving, particularly on significant dates (Rando, 1993). She suggests that creating personalized rituals or adapting existing traditions can provide a sense of continuity and a way to connect with the loved one.

Grief's Impact on Holidays:

J. William Worden discusses how holidays and anniversaries can trigger what he calls "grief bursts," sudden and intense emotional reactions (Worden, 2009). Awareness of this aspect of grief can help individuals and families prepare for and navigate these emotionally charged times.

Navigating Family Dynamics During Holidays:

Kenneth Doka and Terry Martin's work on grieving styles highlights the different ways individuals within a family may experience and express grief during holidays and anniversaries (Doka & Martin, 2010). Recognizing these varying styles can aid in managing family dynamics and supporting each other through these challenging times.

Through exploring research perspectives, we aim to offer insights into the unique challenges presented by holidays, anniversaries, and birthdays in the context of grief. The strategies provided here seek to empower individuals to navigate these significant dates with a sense of purpose and healing.

In concluding this section, we recognize the profound impact that significant dates can have on those in grief. These are challenging times, whether through meeting reluctance about creating new rituals, the nature of grief bursts, or navigating family dynamics. Remember, it is normal for these dates to evoke a range of emotions, and acknowledging and preparing for them can be an essential step in your healing journey.

As you navigate your path through grief, let these insights be a source of comfort and strength, helping you honor your memories while embracing the future with resilience and hope.

Navigating Loss: Suggestions & Support

This part of your journey requires a delicate balance of honoring the past while caring for your present emotional well-being. The actionable tasks here are thoughtfully curated to guide you through these times. From creating new traditions to honoring and remembering your loved one in special ways, each suggestion is aimed at helping you navigate these dates with a sense of purpose and peace. Whether dealing with the mixed emotions that arise or finding ways to remember your loved one, this section offers compassionate strategies and support, knowing that these milestones can be challenging and healing.

Create New Traditions: Consider creating new traditions that honor your loved one while allowing for new experiences and joys.

Honor Your Loved One with an Act of Kindness to Society: Seek out a way to offer your time or a donation that would be important to your loved one. Examples include buying school supplies for a child in the grade your child would be in or volunteering for a group your loved one supported.

Set Realistic Expectations: Understand that it's okay if you don't feel up to large gatherings or festive celebrations. Set realistic expectations for yourself and communicate them to those around you.

Create a Memory Space: On these significant days, consider setting up a small space in your home dedicated to your loved one. This can be a quiet corner with photos, their favorite items, or a book where guests can write memories.

Involve Others in Remembrance: If comfortable, involve friends and family in your acts of remembrance. This could be a group activity like releasing balloons with messages or a communal meal where everyone shares a story about their loved one.

Journal Your Feelings: Write in a journal leading up to and on significant dates. Expressing your thoughts and feelings can help you process your emotions during these emotionally charged times.

Allow for Flexibility: Be flexible with your plans. If you find a certain tradition too painful this year, changing your mind and doing something different or nothing is okay.

Connect with a Support Group: Consider joining a support group to share your feelings and experiences with others who understand what you're going through.

Engage in a Creative Project: Channel your emotions into a creative project, such as making a scrapbook, writing a poem, or creating art that honors your loved one's memory.

Reflect on Positive Memories: While acknowledging the pain, also take time to reflect on the positive memories and the joy that your loved one brought into your life.

Take Time for Reflection: Spend some time in solitude, reflecting on your journey and the presence of your loved one in your life. This can be a time for meditation, prayer, or simply sitting quietly.

Communicate Your Needs: Don't hesitate to communicate your needs to those around you. Let them know how they can best support you during these times.

Plan for Tough Days: Anticipate that these days might be challenging, and plan activities that are comforting or meaningful to you.

Share Memories: Use special days to share stories and memories of your loved one, keeping their spirit a part of your celebrations.

Give Yourself Permission to Feel: Allow yourself to experience a range of emotions. Feeling sadness, joy, or even a mix of both is okay.

Seek and Offer Support: Surround yourself with people who understand and respect your journey, and don't hesitate to reach out for support when you need it and offer it to those on a similar journey.

Honor Your Loved One: Find ways to honor the memory of your loved one, such as lighting a candle or donating in their name.

Practice Self-Care: These days can be emotionally draining. Engage in activities that nourish your soul and bring you peace.

Navigating the calendar is about learning to live with grief during those days that shine a spotlight on your loss. It's about finding a path through these significant dates that respects your grief journey while embracing moments of remembrance and joy.

Acknowledging the personal nature of grieving through holidays, anniversaries, and birthdays is important. The strategies and tasks presented here are meant to serve as a supportive framework, allowing you to navigate these significant dates in a way that feels right for you. Remember, there is no set formula for how you should experience these days. It's about finding a balance that honors your memories while caring for your current emotional needs. Whether you choose to immerse yourself in new traditions, spend time in reflection, or simply allow yourself to feel a range of emotions, know that each step you take is a part of your unique journey of healing. As you move forward, carry with you the knowledge that it's possible to find moments of peace and even joy amidst the challenges of these special dates.

CHAPTER 15

Sacred Spaces: His Room and Belongings

"You can clutch the past so tightly to your chest that it leaves your arms too full to embrace the present." —Jan Glidewell

Before our journey, we never truly understood the power of material things involved in a life cut short. However, this experience also shifted our attachment to our items. For years, we had collectibles, including Kathy's wedding dress, which we had saved. But after Trevor's passing, the significance of that dress in our possession transformed; it meant nothing to us anymore, yet it held immense potential to honor a life in another way. We donated the dress to a group that made burial clothing for babies, finding solace in the thought that it could bring comfort to another family in their time of sorrow.

For those of us grappling with the loss of a loved one, their personal spaces and belongings carry an emotional weight that is profound and deeply felt, more important than our items! These items are tangible connections to the one we deeply miss, each resonating with memories and significance. We often find ourselves at a crossroads, navigating a sea of conflicting emotions when deciding what to do with these treasured possessions and spaces. Should we preserve them just as they were, as enduring tributes to a life cherished and lived? Or should we gently reshape them, finding a way to integrate the reality of our loss into the ongoing tapestry of our lives?

Awareness that the individual's bond with these sacred spaces and belongings is essential for friends and family supporting someone in grief. It's about providing empathetic and pressure-free support, recognizing that each person's approach to these items is deeply personal and unique. This chapter delves into the intricacies of these deeply personal decisions. It offers insights into the emotional journey that accompanies honoring the memory of our loved ones while navigating our path forward amidst their physical absence. It's a guide to finding a balance – between remembrance and resilience, preserving memories and embracing the future. Through our story of repurposing Kathy's wedding dress, we illustrate how transforming our loved ones' belongings can be a profound act of healing and remembrance, a way to extend their legacy and impact meaningfully.

Her Quest for Enlightened Comprehension:

The door to Trevor's room remained closed for months, serving as a silent guardian of a space frozen in time. We often went in there to feel close to him, yet everything stayed just as he left it for almost two years. When I finally gathered the strength to alter something in his room, each step felt like an additional stab in my heart. His room was a snapshot of his six-year-old world – books scattered around, half-assembled LEGOs, and the precious rocks he had joyfully collected outside. It was the perfect scene of a young boy's well-lived life. Sitting on his bed, clutching his pillow, I let the flood of memories and emotions wash over me. It was a space filled with profound connection and intense longing. That was all I could handle for today.

Over the next few months, we continued to visit his room with the intention of tackling a drawer or a shelf. Each time, as soon as it became too overwhelming, we'd step out, acknowledging our limits and knowing that we would try again another day. It took us months to sort through Trevor's belongings little by little. Some things were saved, others were donated. An out-of-state move years later prompted a significant clearing out of material things, but the bin of Trevor's belongings stayed intact and moved with us. It remains a bin that holds not only memories of some difficult days but also of our journey through one of the hardest parts of our lives as a couple, a testament to our determination that this loss would not break us.

His Path of Insightful Realization:

Trevor's room had transformed into a time capsule, where happiness and sorrow were inextricably intertwined. Every object, every corner of the room, held memories – some brought smiles, others tears. The decision to remove items from his room was laden with significance. It felt like a step towards accepting the stark reality of his absence. Yet, paradoxically, keeping his things exactly as he left them sustained a sliver of unrealistic hope, a comforting illusion that he was still a part of our everyday life.

The question that constantly echoed in my mind was how to honor these objects, these fragments of Trevor's life, without letting the sadness they evoked overshadow their value. How could we preserve these items in a way that celebrates his life rather than solely serving as reminders of our loss?

The answer came gradually, through a process of gentle transformation. We decided to convert his room into a shared workspace – a place of creativity and connection for the entire family. This wasn't about erasing his presence; it was about allowing the space to evolve, to continue being a part of our family's life in a new way. Once Trevor's exclusive domain, the room became a symbol of togetherness, a space where memories were cherished, but new ones were also created.

Sorting through Trevor's toys was another emotional journey. We carefully separated the toys the kids enjoyed from those distinctly "Trevor's." This act was more than just a physical sorting; it was an emotional delineation, recognizing the unique bond each of our children had with these shared playthings. The toys that were unequivocally his were gently boxed up, not packed away in forgotten corners, but kept safe for a future moment when we might find the right way to honor them – perhaps passing them on to other children who could find joy in them, just as Trevor did.

Through these actions – converting his room, sorting his toys, boxing up certain items – we navigated the delicate balance of preserving his memory while allowing ourselves and our family space to grow and heal. Each step was a testament to our love for Trevor, a way to keep his spirit alive in our hearts and home, not tethered to sadness but interwoven with the ongoing tapestry of our family's life.

Research Perspectives:

Lovingly attending to the personal spaces and belongings of a loved one who has passed away is fraught with complex emotions. In this section, we'll delve into the insights of leading experts in grief and bereavement, hoping to support you as you navigate this sensitive part of your journey. Here, we examine how personal items and spaces of the loved one can serve as poignant reminders of the loss, integral to the process of mourning and healing. We explore various perspectives on the significance of these belongings, their emotional attachment, and how individuals might choose to honor, preserve, or transform these sacred spaces. This exploration is designed to provide compassionate guidance and insight into one of the most personal aspects of grieving – the relationship with the physical remnants of a loved one's life.

Emotional Attachment to Belongings:

Colin Murray Parkes' studies highlight the emotional attachment to the belongings of the loved one and how they serve as tangible reminders of the person lost (Parkes, 1972). Parkes emphasizes the significance of these items in maintaining a continued bond with the loved one.

The Role of Personal Items in Grieving:

Therese Rando explains that the personal items of the loved one can evoke powerful memories and emotions, playing a crucial role in the grieving process (Rando, 1993). She discusses the importance of these belongings in connecting the bereaved to their lost loved ones.

Transforming Spaces as Part of Grieving:

J. William Worden's work on the tasks of mourning includes the necessity of adapting to an environment without a loved one (Worden, 2009). This can involve transforming the loved one's personal space, a process that can be both painful and healing.

By integrating various research perspectives, it aims to offer insights into the deeply personal decisions regarding the belongings and spaces of the loved one. Maintaining or transforming these spaces can be a significant part of the grieving process. Navigating the personal items and areas of a loved one who has passed is a journey as unique as the individual and their relationship with the loved one. Whether it involves maintaining a connection through preserved rooms and cherished items or finding healing in transforming these spaces, these decisions are deeply personal and integral to the grieving process.

There is no right or wrong way to approach these sacred spaces. Ultimately, how one chooses to interact with the belongings and spaces of a loved one is a reflection of their continuing bond and their unique journey through grief.

Navigating Loss: Suggestions & Support

Here, you will find a range of suggestions designed to respect the emotional significance of your loved one's items and spaces while acknowledging the diverse ways individuals process grief. Whether you are contemplating how to preserve memories, transform spaces, or seek support during this process, this section aims to provide you with thoughtful and caring strategies that can be tailored to your unique situation and needs.

Take Your Time: There's no rush to decide about your loved one's room or belongings. Allow yourself to take the time you need.

Honor Your Emotions: It's normal to feel a range of emotions when dealing with your loved one's belongings. Honor these feelings – they are part of your connection to the person you lost.

Create a Memorial Space: Consider creating a small area in your home dedicated to your loved one's memory, where you can place special items that remind you of them.

Document Memories: If you're not ready to part with items but need to declutter, consider taking photos of them. This way, you can preserve the memories associated with each item without physically keeping everything.

Set Small Goals: Start with manageable tasks, like sorting through a single drawer or a box. Breaking the process into smaller steps can make it feel less overwhelming.

Host a Remembrance Gathering: Invite close friends and family for a remembrance gathering where you can share stories and memories associated with your loved one's belongings. This can be a healing way to honor their memory collectively.

Incorporate Items Into Daily Life: Consider integrating some of your loved one's belongings into your daily life, like using their favorite mug or jewelry. A lamp is one of my favorite items we created from Trevor's belongings. This can be a comforting way to keep their memory close.

Donate to a Cause They Care About: If you donate items, consider donating them to an important cause or organization to your loved one. This can add meaning to the act of letting go.

Write Letters or Messages: If parting with certain items feels particularly difficult, write a letter or a message to your loved one expressing your feelings and the memories associated with the item. This can be a cathartic way to say goodbye.

Create a Memory Box or Scrapbook: Select a few special items to create a memory box or scrapbook. This can be a comforting way to revisit memories in a more contained and organized manner.

Allow for Changing Feelings: Feelings about your loved one's belongings might change over time. Revisiting your decisions and making changes as your healing process evolves is okay.

Involve Family in Decisions: If and when you're ready, involve family members in decisions about what to do with belongings. It can be a shared process of remembering and healing.

Repurpose with Care: If you choose to repurpose or donate items, consider doing so in a way that honors the memory of your loved one. It can be part of the healing process.

Seek Support if Needed: If you find it too difficult to handle your loved one's belongings, don't hesitate to seek support from friends, family, or a grief coach.

We hope that the guidance provided has offered you both comfort and practical approaches to handling the sacred spaces and belongings of your loved one. Remember, navigating through this aspect of grief is a deeply personal journey, and the choices you make are a reflection of your unique relationship with the person you have lost. The suggestions here are intended to be flexible and adaptable to your circumstances, offering support as you make decisions that feel right for you. As you move forward, may you find strength in the knowledge that each step you take in this process is part of honoring your loved one's memory and your path toward healing and reconciliation with your loss.

CHAPTER 16

Embracing Change: Redefining Normal

"The reality is that you will grieve forever. You will not 'get over' the loss of a loved one; you will learn to live with it. You will heal, and you will rebuild yourself around the loss you have suffered. You will be whole again, but you will never be the same. Nor should you be the same, nor would you want to." —Elisabeth Kübler-Ross

If we had to pinpoint how long it took before things felt normal "ish," we'd say it was at least five years. The constant disbelief that Trevor was even gone continued to resonate in a way that made us question our sanity. At times, we were pretty sure we were going mad. This relentless questioning and sense of unreality were a stark reminder of the profound impact of our loss, a testament to how deeply it had rooted itself in our everyday experience. Still, we recognize that life without Trevor, while happy, is still tinged with a sense of incompleteness. This realization is a melancholy reminder of the space he once filled in our lives. We've learned that our journey through grief and finding happiness again doesn't mean forgetting or replacing what we've lost. Instead, it's about learning to carry our love for Trevor alongside our capacity to experience joy, learning that our happiness is now enriched, not diminished, by our memories and love for him.

The poignant phrase "Grief is just love with nowhere to go" captures what many feel when they experience loss. The origin of this phrase is not definitively attributed to any single author, but it has resonated deeply with many who have faced grief. The idea here is that grief, at its core, is an expression of deep love that has lost its primary object. When someone we care for is no longer physically present, the love we hold for them doesn't vanish. Instead, it lingers, searching for expression.

This concept suggests that grief is not something to be moved on from or to be left behind, but rather a profound manifestation of enduring love. It's love that has been displaced, no longer able to be shared with the person who is gone, yet it's still alive and present. This view of grief shifts the perspective from seeing it as a solely painful experience to recognizing it as a complex, bittersweet testament to the strength and depth of our love. In this light, grieving becomes a process of finding a new home for that love – in our memories, in the legacy of the person who has passed, and in the ways we continue to carry them with us in our daily lives. It's about learning to live with the love that remains, allowing it to evolve, and finding ways to honor and express it. This can bring a measure of comfort and meaning to the grieving process, recognizing that the depth of our grief is a measure of the depth of our love.

The concept of "normalcy" after loss is both elusive and complex. For those of us who have experienced profound loss, life is forever altered. This chapter delves into the journey of redefining what a fulfilling life looks like in the wake of such a profound change. It involves acknowledging that the loss remains a part of our story but does not entirely define our future. This journey is about discovering new aspects of ourselves, forming new routines, and finding meaning in a world that has shifted. We learn to weave our experiences of grief into the fabric of a new normal, finding ways to honor our lost loved ones while engaging with life's ongoing opportunities and joys. We come to understand that life can still hold moments of joy, purpose, and fulfillment, even as we carry the weight of our loss.

For those supporting someone in grief, this process of redefining normalcy is crucial. It's about offering patience and empathy as the bereaved navigate this significant transition. Supporters can provide a stable presence, offering encouragement without rushing the process or imposing their expectations of what "moving on" should look like. It involves recognizing that the grieving process may lead to profound changes in the bereaved's personality, interests, and life choices. Support that respects these changes is key, encouraging open communication and showing empathy for their evolving journey through grief. This path of redefining normal is not just about adapting to change but also embracing it, allowing the transformative power of grief to guide us toward a renewed sense of self and purpose.

Her Quest for Enlightened Comprehension:

Finding "normal" often feels like a pursuit of something elusive, especially in the aftermath of profound loss. There are moments when it seems like a lost cause, as if the concept of normalcy has slipped through my fingers, irretrievably altered by the void left behind. The routines and rhythms that once defined my everyday life now seem distant, part of a world that no longer exists in the same way.

In this new landscape of grief, I've found that sometimes it's not so much about actively finding a new normal as it is about letting this new normal find you. It's a subtle, gradual process where moments of clarity and adaptation emerge organically from the chaos of loss. This new normal doesn't arrive with fanfare or a clear roadmap; instead, it seeps into the crevices of life, slowly reshaping my days and understanding of what it means to move forward.

This evolving normalcy is often unexpected in its form and timing. It can surface in small things: finding comfort in a new routine, discovering a previously unknown resilience, or experiencing moments of joy that once seemed impossible. In these moments, I realize a new normal has begun to weave itself into the fabric of my life, quietly and persistently.

Embracing this new normal doesn't mean forgetting the past or the pain of loss. Instead, it's about allowing myself to evolve and grow in the face of change. It's acknowledging that while life will never be the same, it can still be rich and meaningful in transformed ways. In this journey, I learn to balance the act of remembering with the act of living, creating a life that honors the past while embracing the possibilities of the present and the future.

This new normal is not something I chose, but it's something I'm learning to live with. It's a testament to the enduring impact of love and loss and the incredible capacity of the human spirit to adapt and find a way forward, even in the midst of grief.

His Path of Insightful Realization:

The phrase "our new normal" became a way to encapsulate our life after Trevor's death. It was a life marked by his absence – the silence where his voice should have been, the altered dynamics as we watched the children interact without their brother, one less mouth to feed at the dinner table, the absence of his playful bargaining over dessert. I couldn't help but mourn the future we wouldn't see, the impossibility of watching Trevor grow up and discover who he would become. Life seemed to slow down, enveloped in a more profound quietness than a mere lack of sound. Smiles became rare in our household, and laughter – once a frequent visitor – now felt like a stranger, tentative and sparse.

Over time, however, this "new normal" began to evolve. It turned into something more guarded and reserved, yes, but also something that could accommodate remembrance and joy. We learned to find laughter in our happy memories of Trevor, allowing these moments to lighten our hearts. It became important to show our children that death, though a painful part of life, shouldn't overshadow living. We started to venture out into the world again, going on vacations, but always taking a part of Trevor with us by carrying his ashes. This way, he was still a part of our family adventures in a different yet meaningful way.

Launching Trevor's Toes and Tushies 501(c)(3), a project dedicated to his memory, allowed us to keep his warm heart and caring nature alive and share it with others. It became a channel for us to transform our sorrow into support for ourselves and the community. This initiative was a way to celebrate Trevor's life and impact, keeping his spirit present in our daily activities.

Simultaneously, we shifted our focus to providing for the needs of our living children. Giving them the support and space they needed to move forward and rediscover joy in life was crucial. This meant creating an environment where they could freely express their grief, ask questions, and find their paths to healing.

In this new normal, we found a balance between honoring Trevor's memory and embracing the lives we still had to live. It was a delicate, ongoing process of shifting gears from mourning to living, a journey of finding meaning and joy amidst the shadows of loss.

Research Perspectives:

This section draws upon the expertise of renowned grief and bereavement researchers whose work has profoundly contributed to our comprehension of how individuals and families navigate the transformation of their "normal" after experiencing a significant loss. This section aims to connect theory with practice, providing a research-backed foundation for the experiences and challenges you may be facing. We explore various studies and ideas illuminating the journey of redefining normalcy in the wake of grief. We offer insights into the psychological processes, emotional adjustments, and the potential for growth and change that can arise during this complex time. Here, you will find a synthesis of research that not only informs but also supports and validates your personal experience of embracing a new normal after a loss.

The Process of Creating a New Normal:

Colin Murray Parkes' work on bereavement highlights the necessity of adapting to a new life after a loss (Parkes, 1972). He discusses how bereaved individuals gradually come to terms with their changed reality, a process that often involves redefining their sense of normalcy.

Growth and Transformation in Grief:

Therese Rando's research emphasizes the potential for personal growth and transformation following a loss (Rando, 1993). She identifies the process of developing a new normal as an opportunity for the bereaved to rediscover themselves and forge a path forward.

Adapting to Change After Loss:

J. William Worden's "tasks of mourning" concept includes finding an enduring connection with the loved one while adjusting to a new reality

(Worden, 2009). This adaptation is a crucial step in forming a new sense of normalcy.

Continuing Bonds and New Identities:

Kenneth Doka and Terry Martin's studies on continuing bonds show how maintaining a connection with the loved one can coexist with developing a new identity and lifestyle post-loss (Doka & Martin, 2010). This balance is key in redefining what normalcy means after grief.

The research and theories from leading experts in the field provide a deeper comprehension of the multifaceted nature of this transition. These perspectives highlight the variety of ways individuals process change, cope with loss, and ultimately find a path forward. This body of work underscores the importance of acknowledging and embracing the changes that come with loss, suggesting potential for personal growth, newfound resilience, and a redefined sense of fulfillment through this challenging process. We hope the insights provided in this section offer both validation and guidance as you navigate your path through grief, helping you understand that while the journey is uniquely yours, it is also shared by many others who have walked similar paths. Through integrating these research perspectives, this chapter provides insights into the challenging yet potentially transformative journey of redefining normalcy after a loss. It offers guidance for those navigating this complex aspect of grief, emphasizing the importance of personal growth, adaptation, and maintaining a continuing bond with the loved one.

Navigating Loss: Suggestions & Support

This part of the chapter offers practical strategies and empathetic guidance as you navigate the challenging process of finding or allowing a new normal to emerge. Here, we will explore various approaches to embracing change, from establishing new routines to finding unexpected sources of joy and meaning. This section is crafted to support you in this transformation phase, providing tools and suggestions that respect the complexity of your grief journey. Whether taking small steps towards redefining your day-to-day life or seeking deeper changes to rediscover fulfillment, these insights help guide and uplift you on your path toward healing and growth.

Embrace the Journey of Self-Discovery: Give yourself permission to explore new interests, hobbies, and passions. This can be a path to rediscovering joy and purpose.

Be Open to Change in Relationships: Recognize that some relationships may evolve or change as you navigate your grief. Embrace supportive and empathetic connections.

Reflect on Your Values and Goals: Reflect on what is truly important to you now. Your loss may have shifted your perspective, and it's okay to realize and acknowledge your values have changed, too.

Accept the Fluidity of Grief: Understand that grief is not linear and that your journey toward a new normal will have ups and downs.

Create New Routines: Establish new routines that provide structure and comfort while allowing room for the memories and presence of your loved one.

Explore New Interests: Consider exploring new hobbies or activities that can bring a sense of fulfillment and joy, opening pathways to new experiences.

Honor Your Loved One in Daily Life: Find small ways to incorporate the memory of your loved one into your daily life, whether through rituals, storytelling, or keeping certain traditions alive.

Connect with Others: Maintain connections with supportive friends and family, and consider joining support groups to share your experiences with others who understand. Finding others who understand your experience can be incredibly validating.

Seek Professional Support: If you find it challenging to navigate your changing world, don't hesitate to seek support from a grief coach or therapist.

Remember, redefining normalcy after a loss is a deeply personal process that unfolds at its own pace and in its unique way. The ideas and suggestions presented in this section are meant to be a starting point, a source of inspiration as you explore what change looks like for you. We encourage you to adapt these ideas to fit your needs and circumstances, always remembering that your journey of healing and rediscovery is yours alone. May this section serve as a compassionate companion, guiding you toward a life that, while forever changed, can still hold beauty, purpose, and joy.

CHAPTER 17

Navigating Grief's Isolation and Relationship Changes

"No one ever told me that grief felt so like fear."
—C. S. Lewis

P eople who saw us after Trevor passed seemed to be afraid of us, perhaps apprehensive because they didn't know what to say or how to act around our grief. This fear, often rooted in a lack of understanding of how to approach someone in deep mourning, contributed to our feelings of isolation.

By using empathetic language, society can play a crucial role in bridging the isolation often felt by those in grief. Here are some examples of what people could say to show empathy:

"I'm so sorry for your loss. I'm here if you need to talk or even just sit in silence."

"I can't imagine how you're feeling, but I want you to know I'm here to support you in any way I can."

"It's okay to feel however you're feeling right now. There's no right or wrong way to grieve."

"I've been thinking about you a lot and wanted to check in. How are you doing right now?" The emphasis is on how they feel right now, not "today," which could have varied 100 times already.

"I remember you mentioning how much you loved [specific memory or trait of the loved one]. I'd love to hear more about that when you're ready."

"Take all the time you need. I'm here for you now and in the future, whenever you're ready."

"I don't have the right words to make this better, but I want you to know that I care deeply and am here to listen."

"Is there anything specific I can do to help you right now? I'm willing to be there in whatever way you need."

"It's okay not to be okay. I'm here to support you through this, no matter what."

"I can only imagine how hard this is for you. Please know that you're not alone, and I'm just a phone call away if you need anything."

"Your feelings are valid, no matter what they are. I'm here to listen whenever you want to share."

"I can't fully understand what you're going through, but I'm here to help you in any way you need."

"If you ever feel like getting out of the house or need a change of scenery, I'm here. We can do whatever feels comfortable for you."

"I don't want to intrude on your grief, but I want you to know I am thinking of you and am here for you."

"I'm here for the long haul, not just now but in the weeks and months ahead when you might need support."

"If you need someone to handle practical things like errands or appointments, I'm more than willing to help."

"I wish I had the right words. Just know I care deeply and am here for you in any way you need."

"Please don't hesitate to let me know how I can make things easier for you during this time."

"I understand if you're not up for talking. Just know I'm always here to listen whenever you are ready."

"It's perfectly okay not to be strong all the time. I'm here to lean on whenever you need."

"I can only imagine the pain you're going through, and I'm here to provide a shoulder to cry on or an ear to listen."

"Remember, taking things one day at a time is okay. I'm here to walk alongside you every step of the way."

"I'm always just a phone call away if you need to talk or if you need silence but don't want to be alone."

"I'm here to support you, whether it's a late-night call or just sitting together in silence. You're not alone in this."

These responses convey empathy, respect the unique experience of the grieving individual, and offer support without making assumptions about what the person might need or feel. They help create a sense of connection, which can be incredibly valuable for anyone in grief.

We always wanted people to know that bringing Trevor up wouldn't remind us of him. That mentioning Trevor doesn't bring us unexpected pain. The truth is, thoughts of him are always with us, like a continuous loop in our minds. When others talk about Trevor, it brings us comfort rather than sorrow. It reassures us that his presence was real and meaningful in the lives of others, too. Hearing these memories and stories from friends and family helps us feel connected to the reality of his impact and keeps his spirit alive in our shared experiences.

For many of us, grief can feel like walking a path that no one else can truly understand. This section delves into the feelings of loneliness and disconnection accompanying loss, offering strategies to manage this solitude. It's about finding ways to bridge the gap between the need for space and connection, learning that solitude in grief can be both a sanctuary and a prison. The reluctance of others to engage, often stemming from their uncertainty and fear, can deepen the sense of isolation for those who are grieving.

For those supporting someone in grief, recognizing the isolating aspects of their experience is crucial. This part of the chapter discusses how supporters can empathize with the bereaved's need for solitude while providing a presence that reassures them they are not alone. It's about offering support that respects the griever's space and gently reminds them that they are still connected to a world that cares. Navigating this delicate balance can help alleviate the isolation of grief and reinforce the bonds of empathy and compassion.

For further guidance on supporting others through their grief, delve into Chapter 1, "Supporting Others in Grief: Empathetic Connection and Compassion," which offers clear strategies for prioritizing support in the initial days following a loss, and Chapter 10, "Navigating Social Currents and Keeping My Radar Clean in a World of Hurt," providing insights into understanding the day-to-day reality of grief and how it shapes one's experience and interactions.

Her Quest for Enlightened Comprehension:

In writing this book, I reflect on a profound and painful reality: my extended family has endured the loss of not just one but two cherished children. Each loss has been accompanied by significant rifts within our family, adding layers of complexity to our grief. The first time this happened, the challenge was immense for my husband and me. I remember screaming inside, "How can you not see this as only making this situation harder?" We were grappling with the devastating loss of Trevor, and the additional strain of family disputes made it even more overwhelming. At that time, my primary focus was to stay afloat for my two younger children. Trevor's sudden passing was a stark reminder of life's unpredictability. I had to retreat into a space removed from family, not because I didn't love them, but because I could not carry both my grief and the conflict. Losing Trevor reinforced my belief in living without regret and the harmfulness of harboring internal anger, so our families eventually recovered, and life moved forward.

When a similar situation unfolded with the second loss, it struck me profoundly, prompting a deeper exploration into these family dynamics.

Grief often leads to depleted resources, misunderstandings, and mismatched expectations. Actions taken from this place of scarcity can inadvertently cause more distress rather than providing support. This is why I emphasize the importance of taking a moment to pause. Viktor Frankl's profound words in *Man's Search for Meaning* resonate deeply with me: "When we can no longer change a situation, we are challenged to change ourselves... Everything can be taken from a human but one thing: the last of the human freedoms—to choose one's attitude in any given set of circumstances, to choose one's own way" (Frankl, 1946). Frankl discovered an "inner freedom" in his response to the direst circumstances, a lesson in choosing our responses instead of being dictated by circumstances. This principle guides me to pause, reflect, and consciously choose how to proceed in relationships, whether with anger or compassion, support or separation. But the pause is critical for choosing the intention and then the action!

Despite these challenges within my family, I firmly believe keeping the door open for reconciliation is essential and worth pursuing. The unpredictability of life, especially evident in the face of sudden loss, also signifies the potential for change – in situations, in others, and within ourselves. My belief that people can change, heal, transform, and grow informs my approach to family dynamics, especially in conflict. I advocate for open, empathetic, honest communication, allowing space and time as needed, and addressing conflicts with a forgiving mindset. It's about recognizing our shared humanity, navigating life's complexities as best we can with empathy, and stopping to choose our intention in our next action! It's not about dismissing the pain or impact of past actions; instead, it's about finding paths toward healing and potentially building stronger, more understanding relationships.

Throughout our lives, each of us is subject to a complex conditioning process. This conditioning comes from our upbringing, societal norms, past experiences, and even the media. It shapes our beliefs, attitudes, and behaviors, often operating beneath our conscious awareness. While this conditioning can help guide our responses in many situations, it can also lead us astray, especially in complex emotional scenarios. For instance, in times of stress or grief, our conditioned responses might manifest as withdrawal, anger, or even misplaced blame. Understanding this can bring a degree of compassion – for ourselves and others – when we react in ways that we later regret or don't fully understand. It's essential to recognize that much of our automatic, instinctive reactions to situations are a product of this deep-seated conditioning.

To address this conditioning, we first need to become aware of it. This involves mindful reflection and self-awareness, taking a step back, again a pause, to observe our reactions and asking ourselves why we respond in certain ways. Are our actions genuinely reflective of our values or remnants of past conditioning?

Once we identify these conditioned patterns, we can start the work of reconditioning – actively choosing responses after a pause that aligns more closely with our current values and knowledge. This process isn't easy and doesn't happen overnight. It requires patience, continuous self-reflection, and, often, the willingness to seek external support, such as therapy, counseling, or coaching.

In conversations and interactions, especially in emotionally charged situations, pausing and reflecting are beneficial. Ask yourself: "Is my response driven by old conditioning, or is it a conscious choice based on the person I am today?" This pause can make a significant difference, allowing space for more thoughtful, empathetic, and effective communication.

Recognizing and addressing our conditioning is about evolving and growing as individuals. It's about ensuring that our actions and reactions reflect who we are now and who we aspire to be, rather than just echoes of our past conditioning.

Embracing this mindset is a step toward personal peace. It involves a conscious decision not to let anger take hold but instead to focus our energies on fostering growth and harmony, even if it is only for ourselves initially. As we evolve individually, so can our relationships, opening up possibilities for deeper connections to each other's experiences and viewpoints.

In the complex dance of family dynamics, there comes a time when entanglement can twist into estrangement. The lack of empathy, the absence of shared sorrow, or simply the divergent paths our grief journeys take can lead to a chasm that feels too wide to bridge. I would find myself puzzled, feeling isolated in my pain, until I remember their reality doesn't align with mine. The lens through which they see life doesn't include the soul-crushing weight of holding their deceased child in their arms, a memory that greets me each morning with aching clarity. This disparity in experiences creates a divide that's difficult to articulate and even harder to bridge, yet it's a stark reminder of how uniquely personal grief can be.

His Path of Insightful Realization:

In the quiet of our living room, where the lively pulse of family life once resonated, a profound stillness has taken root since Trevor's passing. This heavy, almost palpable silence starkly contrasts with the days when friends filled our home with joy and conversation. Their gradual withdrawal left me enveloped in a solitude born from grief, comforting in its familiarity yet oppressively isolating.

As I reflected on these silent moments, I realized the isolating nature of grief. It distances us from the world and strains our closest relationships. Many friends, once central to our lives, seemed to drift away. I pondered whether the rawness of our grief was overwhelming for them or if it was merely the natural progression of life, with people drifting in and out. Those who remained often shared a similar loss, creating a bond born of mutual appreciation for our experiences. Equally valuable were those who stayed despite not having faced such loss themselves; their unwavering presence affirmed the resilience and strength of enduring relationships.

In connecting with other parents who had also lost a child, there was an unspoken understanding and ease in our interactions. These connections formed naturally, contrasting with the more strained conversations with those who hadn't faced such a loss. Interactions with them often felt guarded, hindered by a barrier of unspoken fear and unfamiliarity with such depths of loss. It was as if their mindset of "it won't happen to me" created a chasm in our mutual understanding.

Grief also manifested differently within my marriage, affecting how my wife and I processed our emotions and responded to each other's needs. Navigating these differences required patience and empathy. I learned to support my wife in her unique journey through grief, consciously setting aside any frustration over unmet needs. Realizing that grief initially brought a tunnel vision, narrowing my focus to my pain and inadvertently overlooking the needs of those around me.

However, this tunnel vision began to recede with time, gradually broadening my perspective. I became more attuned to the experiences and needs of others in my family and community. This shift was slow but instrumental in helping me adapt to the altered dynamics of my relationships. It marked a crucial step in the healing journey, allowing me to extend my empathy beyond my grief.

Research Perspectives:

Here, we offer a deeper comprehension of the complexities surrounding the isolation often experienced in grief and the profound ways in which relationships are impacted by loss. Drawing from a rich pool of research, we explore how grief can create barriers to communication and connection and the varied responses of individuals and communities to the bereaved. This section bridges the gap between personal experiences and scholarly insights, providing a well-rounded perspective on how grief influences internal solitude and external social dynamics. By integrating these research perspectives, we aim to provide support and validation for the diverse experiences of those navigating the solitary journey of grief and the evolving dance of relationships during such transformative times.

Grief-Related Isolation:

Colin Murray Parkes' research on bereavement highlights the isolating nature of grief, noting how the loss of a significant person can lead to feelings of loneliness and disconnection from others (Parkes, 1972). Parkes emphasizes recognizing these feelings as a natural part of the grieving process.

Impact of Grief on Family Dynamics:

Research has shown that grief can significantly impact family dynamics and relationships. According to a study by Klass and Walter (2001), a family member's death can alter the family's relational equilibrium, sometimes leading to strained relationships. These strains may arise from differing grieving styles, unmet emotional needs, or unresolved conflicts that resurface during the grieving process. Therese Rando's studies delve into how grief can alter one's relationships, including shifts in family dynamics and friendships (Rando, 1993). She discusses the importance of navigating these changes with sensitivity and awareness, acknowledging how grief can affect interpersonal connections.

Family Entanglements and Relationship Changes, Including Estrangement:

Family entanglements during grief often involve complex emotional interactions. As Hooyman and Kramer (2006) note, these can include feelings of guilt, resentment, or blame, which can intensify existing family tensions. The end of some relationships may occur due to the inability to navigate these heightened emotions and differing needs during grief.

Family entanglements, characterized by complex and emotionally charged relationships, can significantly impact individual well-being and development. These entanglements often stem from interactions with emotionally immature individuals (Gibson, 2015; 2019), who may struggle with recognizing and respecting boundaries, leading to a pervasive impact across various relationships. Emotionally immature individuals often create dynamics where the emotional needs and boundaries of others are not adequately recognized or respected, blurring lines and impeding the development of healthy, independent identities in those around them. These patterns of emotional immaturity can be deeply ingrained, often reflecting behaviors and coping mechanisms passed down through generations. While these behaviors are not isolated to parent-child dynamics, they can manifest in any relationship where emotional immaturity plays a central role.

Specifically focusing on the parent-child aspect, the impact of emotionally immature parents on their children can be profound and long-lasting (Gibson, 2015; 2019). In these relationships, parents may oscillate between being overly involved in certain aspects of their children's lives and neglectful in others, leading to confusion and emotional turmoil for the child. This dynamic affects the immediate relationship between the parent and child and sets a precedent for how the child navigates relationships in the future, potentially perpetuating a cycle of emotional immaturity across generations. Gibson (2015; 2019) emphasizes the significance of understanding multi-generational influences and how behaviors and emotional patterns from previous generations can impact current family dynamics. This historical perspective offers valuable insights into the root causes of current issues, enabling individuals to break cycles of dysfunction.

Jackson MacKenzie (2019) addresses the impact of toxic family patterns, emphasizing how these entanglements often result in the loss of self-identity and personal boundaries. He suggests recognizing and actively working to break free from these patterns is crucial for reclaiming one's sense of self and establishing healthier relational boundaries. MacKenzie's work highlights the importance of self-awareness and intentional action in disentangling oneself from harmful family dynamics.

Furthermore, Carter (2004) explores the role of invalidation in family relationships, a common feature in toxic family entanglements. He describes how invalidating behaviors from family members, such as manipulation, criticism, or emotional abuse, contribute to a detrimental family environment. Carter advocates for developing coping strategies and assertive communication skills to counter these behaviors, thereby protecting one's self-esteem and emotional health in the face of family entanglements.

Estrangement within families is complex and multifaceted, often resulting from longstanding conflicts, differences in values, or harmful behaviors. Estrangement can occur between family members, not just between parents and children. Jackson MacKenzie (2019) discusses how estrangement can be a necessary boundary in cases of toxic relationships, where continuous interaction leads to emotional harm. It's a form of self-preservation that allows individuals to protect their mental and emotional well-being. Similarly, Lindsay Gibson (2015; 2019) explores how individuals may choose estrangement as a response to dealing with emotionally immature family members. This decision is often made after prolonged efforts to establish healthy boundaries and meaningful communication have failed. Estrangement, in this context, is seen not as an act of rejection but as an assertion of self-respect and the necessity of prioritizing one's mental health. It's important to note that estrangement is often complicated and painful, laden with societal stigma and internal conflict. Yet, it can also be a step towards healing and personal growth, allowing individuals to build healthier relationships and break cycles of emotional dysfunction.

Understanding and addressing family entanglements or estrangement is vital to personal development and emotional well-being. It involves recognizing and navigating the complexities of familial relationships, setting and maintaining personal boundaries, and developing coping strategies to manage and potentially transform these entanglements into healthier dynamics. An essential aspect of this process is seeking clarity on family patterns that may extend back a few generations. This historical perspective offers valuable insights into the root causes of current issues, enabling individuals to break cycles of dysfunction. By exploring and acknowledging the familial legacy, one can better understand their role within the family system and make more informed choices about their relationships and boundaries. This level of understanding is crucial for healing from past traumas and building healthier, more fulfilling family relationships.

The Role of Social Support in Grieving:

J. William Worden's work includes the importance of social support during the grieving process (Worden, 2009). He highlights how the presence or absence of support can significantly influence one's experience of grief and the ability to adapt to life after loss. A research review by Stroebe, Schut, and Stroebe (2005) underscores the vital role of social support in coping with grief, revealing that assistance from friends and the wider community can be just as essential as familial support. This becomes particularly significant in situations where grief leads to strained or lost family relationships. According to a study by Gilat and Shahar (2007), online support forums and communities offer an accessible, immediate, and anonymous form of support. This type of support can be indispensable for those who feel isolated in their grief due to family entanglements or the loss of familial relationships. These avenues provide alternative sources of comfort and connection, helping individuals navigate the complexities of grief when traditional family support systems may not be available or sufficient.

Continuing Bonds and Evolving Relationships:

Kenneth Doka and Terry Martin's concept of "continuing bonds" extends to how maintaining a connection with the loved one can coexist with adapting to changes in relationships with the living (Doka & Martin, 2010). They explore how these bonds can provide comfort and a sense of ongoing connection, even as relationships with others evolve in the wake of loss. This concept counters the traditional notion that moving on from grief requires letting go or detaching from the person who has died. Instead, it suggests that forming a new, different relationship with the memory and legacy of the loved one can be a healthy part of coping with loss.

By integrating these research perspectives, this chapter offers insights into the dual challenges of grief-related isolation and changing relationships. It guides those navigating the solitude often accompanying loss and the complexities of evolving relationships.

Navigating Loss: Suggestions & Support

Here are some actionable strategies to help you manage the dual challenges of feeling isolated in your grief and experiencing shifts in your relationships. This section is designed to be a supportive resource, acknowledging the unique and often solitary path of grief and the dynamic changes in personal relationships following a loss. Whether you are seeking ways to cope with feelings of loneliness or looking for advice on adapting to the evolving nature of your relationships, the suggestions here are tailored to offer comfort and direction. From enhancing communication with loved ones to finding new forms of social support, these strategies are intended to empower you to navigate these aspects of grief with greater understanding and resilience.

Embrace the Evolving Nature of Relationships: Understand that relationships will change and evolve as you navigate your grief and that this is a natural part of the process.

Communicate Openly: Encourage open communication about your needs and feelings with family and friends, and be open to hearing theirs. This can involve setting aside time for family discussions where everyone can express their feelings and perspectives. When conflicts arise, address them constructively. Focus on understanding each other's viewpoints rather than assigning blame. Consider family counseling or coaching to facilitate these conversations in a neutral and supportive environment.

Recognize Individual Grieving Styles: Understand that each family member may grieve differently. Acknowledge and respect these differences to avoid misunderstandings and conflicts. Provide education about how people grieve to foster mutual understanding and tolerance.

Foster Emotional Support: Cultivate a supportive environment where family members feel safe to express their emotions. Engage in joint activities that promote bonding and shared experiences, such as memorializing the loved one.

Accepting Relationship Changes: Acknowledge that some relationships may change or end as a result of grief. Accepting these changes can be a part of the healing process. Seek external support, such as support groups, for dealing with the loss of certain relationships.

Building a Chosen Family or Support Network: Sometimes, friends, colleagues, or community members can provide the empathy and support that one's biological family might not. Building relationships with these individuals can create a chosen family that offers emotional support.

Acknowledge Your Feelings of Loneliness: Recognize and accept your feelings of loneliness as a valid part of your grief journey. Learning that it's okay to feel isolated at times can be a step towards managing these emotions more effectively.

Create a Safe Space for Grieving: Designate a space in your home where you can grieve privately. This can be a quiet corner for reflection, reading, or being with your thoughts and emotions.

Explore New Ways of Socializing: Experiment with different ways of socializing that feel comfortable for you. This could be joining online forums, attending community events, or simply having a coffee with a close friend.

Set Boundaries with Others: Learn to set healthy boundaries in your interactions. Communicate clearly what you are comfortable with and what you are not, especially in social settings or conversations about your loss.

Journal Your Thoughts and Feelings: Maintain a journal to express your thoughts and feelings about how your relationships are changing. This can help you process your emotions and gain clarity.

Plan for Alone Time: Intentionally plan for alone time to process your grief. Balance this with times of social interaction to maintain a healthy equilibrium between solitude and socializing.

Engage in Activities That Nourish You: Participate in nourishing and fulfilling activities. This could be a hobby, exercise, or self-expression that helps you feel connected to yourself.

Seek Supportive Communities: Find support groups or communities where you can share your experiences with others who understand the nuances of grief.

Redefine Connections: Be open to redefining your connections with others, recognizing that some relationships may grow stronger while others may fade.

Prioritize Self-Care: Remember to prioritize your emotional and mental well-being, as this will impact your ability to engage in and maintain healthy relationships.

When Entanglement Becomes Estrangement

Acknowledge Past Patterns: Acknowledging past patterns is a crucial step in personal growth and healing, especially when it comes to relationships. This process involves a thorough introspection and recognition of one's history, particularly identifying the recurring themes or patterns in relationships that have led to pain or discomfort. In *Whole Again* (2019), Jackson MacKenzie emphasizes the importance of this self-awareness, noting that it's essential to understand one's vulnerabilities and triggers to avoid falling into similar harmful situations in the future.

Set and Maintain Boundaries: Setting personal boundaries is an extension of awareness. Defining and maintaining personal boundaries is crucial to establishing what behaviors are acceptable and what are not. This clarity helps assert oneself and ensure that past mistakes are not repeated. Boundaries are about saying no to others and affirming one's values, limits, and rights (Gibson, 2015; 2019).

Trust Your Intuition: Trusting your intuition is fundamental to self-care and decision-making. Intuition often serves as an internal alert system, signaling when something isn't right or a situation might be harmful. In *Whole Again* (2019), Jackson MacKenzie discusses the importance of honoring your inner feelings and instincts, especially after experiences in toxic relationships. He suggests that intuition can be a powerful guide in making decisions that protect your emotional and mental well-being. Intuition, in this sense, is more than just a gut feeling; it's an accumulation of subconscious observations and experiences that inform your reaction to current situations.

Gaining Self-Respect and Building Independent Self-Esteem: Create a balance of power in relationships by standing up to invalidating behaviors and asserting your worth. Building self-esteem independently of others' opinions is critical to valuing oneself without seeking external validation.

Practice Observing and Managing Interactions Deliberately: In relationships where emotional intimacy may not be possible, maintain a state of "relatedness" while managing interactions to respect your needs and desires.

Accepting Limitations of Others and Choosing an Active Self: Recognize and accept the limitations of others for self-protection and emotional health. Understanding that some people may not change their behavior is vital for self-protection and emotional health. Shift from a passive, suffering self to an active, self-advocating stance, focusing on your well-being and avoiding enabling behaviors (Gibson). The concept of choosing an "active self" involves taking proactive steps toward recovery and personal growth instead of remaining in a "suffering self" state, which is often characterized by passivity and victimhood.

Explore the Historical Context of Extended Family: Investigate family patterns that extend back generations. Understanding these multi-generational influences can provide insights into family dynamics, helping break dysfunctional cycles and build healthier relationships.

Prioritize Self-Care: Engage in activities promoting well-being and offering respite from family stress. Prioritizing self-care is essential in managing family entanglements and estrangement.

Seek Professional Help if Needed: Consider coaching or counseling for understanding complex family dynamics, including multi-generational patterns.

Maintain Open Communication Where Possible: Keep the lines of communication open with your family when feasible, expressing feelings and concerns honestly but respectfully.

We hope this journey through the dual challenges of solitude and evolving relationships in grief has been enlightening and supportive. As we have traversed the often lonely path of grieving, we've uncovered ways to embrace solitude while seeking connection. Simultaneously, we have navigated the complexities of how relationships transform in the wake of loss, learning how to adapt to these changes with grace. This journey has also brought to light the difficult reality of estrangement that can accompany grief. Recognizing and empathizing with the pain of estrangement adds another layer to our understanding of loss. It demands a deep sense of empathy, both for ourselves and for those we might become estranged from, as we grapple with grief's multifaceted impact. It can also offer opportunities for growth, deeper connections, and a renewed appreciation of our needs and boundaries, recognizing that each step is part of a broader journey toward healing, self-discovery, and empowerment. May the insights and strategies provided here empower you to find balance in your solitude and strength in your relationships as you continue to navigate the ever-changing landscape of life after loss.

CHAPTER 18

The Weight of Expectations: Societal and Self-Imposed

"They tell us to 'get over,' 'move on,' but they don't understand that we are forever altered." —Unknown

The general discomfort that society exhibits towards grief is indeed a perplexing phenomenon. Despite the fact that grief is an inescapable part of the human experience, with every person encountering loss at some point, there's a widespread reluctance to confront or discuss it openly. This aversion often stems from cultural attitudes that view grief as something to be quickly overcome, a private matter, or even a sign of weakness.

Societal unease with grief manifests in various ways, including the avoidance of discussions about death and loss and expectations that those grieving should "move on" or "get over" their grief within a certain timeframe. There's a tendency to gloss over the pain and complexity of the grieving process, often resulting in offering platitudes instead of genuine support and shying away from the raw emotions that accompany loss.

This discomfort is also evident in the lack of formal rituals or support systems for the bereaved beyond the immediate aftermath of a loss. In many cultures, the mourning period is brief, after which there is an unspoken expectation that normal life should resume. This societal narrative fails to acknowledge the enduring nature of grief and how the loss of a loved one can fundamentally alter a person's life.

The reluctance of society to accommodate and openly discuss grief might be partly due to fear – fear of confronting mortality, fear of deep emotional pain, or fear of not knowing how to respond to someone else's grief. This not only isolates those in mourning but also perpetuates misunderstanding and avoidance around the topic of grief.

Recognizing and addressing this societal discomfort with grief is crucial. By fostering open dialogues, creating supportive communities, and reevaluating cultural norms surrounding grief and mourning, we can shift towards a more compassionate and empathetic approach to this fundamental human experience.

Grievers often face societal norms and self-imposed standards that conflict with their genuine feelings and needs. We encourage critical examination and challenging these norms and standards, advocating for a true grief path to one's authentic emotions and experiences.

Supporters have a crucial role here in helping shift this trend. Providing a judgment-free environment is essential. The chapter emphasizes that the best help friends, family, and the community can offer is assistance without preset norms and expectations. Recognizing that grief is an intensely individual experience, effective support is often rooted in being present and accepting without condition. By challenging societal expectations and embracing a more personalized approach to grief, we can offer meaningful support to those navigating the complexities of loss.

Her Quest for Enlightened Comprehension:

I recall a conversation with a well-meaning person a few months after Trevor's passing. "You're so strong," she said admiringly. "I can't imagine getting through what you have without falling apart." Her words, meant as praise, felt like shackles. There was an unspoken expectation that strength meant not showing my pain, not crumbling under the weight of my grief. It was a societal script on how to grieve "appropriately," and I felt trapped by it. This interaction sparked a realization: the grief journey is often cluttered with expectations – some from society, others we impose upon ourselves. These expectations can become a heavy burden, dictating how we 'should' process our loss. As I write, nine years after Trevor's passing, I see so many ways I harshly judged myself and struggled with how to proceed. Knowing now what I do about grief and its impact on health, I realize the immense strain I put on myself could have had dire consequences.

For this reason, education and supportive presence are vital to allow grief to be in motion – perhaps never fully resolved, but always flowing and processing. I never want to hold anyone on a pedestal for being strong in their grief. There can be resilience, but it's crucial to understand that this resilience coexists with vulnerability, pain, and the need for support.

Grief is a journey that requires compassion from others and ourselves, not a race to be stoically endured. Embracing this perspective is key to navigating the weight of societal and self-imposed expectations and moving towards a path of healing that honors our true feelings and experiences.

His Path of Insightful Realization:

Society often imposes an unspoken rule that mourning should have a time limit, a belief that life should return to normal soon after the funeral rites are concluded. This societal expectation is mirrored in the workplace, where bereavement leave is typically limited to a mere 1–3 days. For those not directly touched by the loss, life swiftly resumes its regular rhythm, as if the death were merely a brief pause. The prevailing attitude seems to be that "the show must go on," regardless of the emotional turmoil beneath.

However, for those of us who have experienced the loss, especially the loss of a child, the reality is starkly different. The bereavement process requires time, far more than society often acknowledges. The void left by a loved one's death is not something that can be quickly filled or ignored. In the case of child loss, this void is profound, creating an imbalance that disrupts life's natural order. Parents are not meant to outlive their children, and when this natural sequence is disrupted, it takes significant time to integrate this reality into the ongoing narrative of our lives.

This transition can be mind-numbing as parents grapple with an event that defies the expected timeline of life. Accepting this altered reality is gradual and deeply personal. It challenges us to come to terms with a fundamental truth: death is an inevitable part of life, and it does not conform to our desired timelines or expectations.

Ultimately, we learn that grief has its own pace, one that societal norms or time frames cannot dictate. It's a journey of coming to terms with loss in a way that honors our emotions and the memory of our loved ones. This journey calls for patience and the acknowledgment that grief is as individual as the bond we share with the person we have lost.

Research Perspectives:

In exploring how societal and self-imposed expectations influence grief, we delve into the cultural norms surrounding grief, the personal standards individuals often grapple with, and the intricate balance between resilience and vulnerability in the face of loss. This section offers a critical overview of the various expectations that can heavily impact those in mourning, providing a deeper awareness of the complexities involved. By integrating academic research with personal experiences of grief, we aim to present a comprehensive perspective to our readers. This approach validates individual grief journeys and challenges conventional narratives about mourning and recovery. We strive to offer insights that acknowledge the multifaceted nature of grief and the diverse ways it can be experienced and expressed.

Societal Expectations in Grief:

Colin Murray Parkes' seminal work on bereavement underscores the societal expectations around grief, noting how cultural norms often dictate a "proper" way to grieve (Parkes, 1972). He emphasizes the diversity of grief experiences and the importance of recognizing these differences rather than adhering to societal prescriptions.

Self-Imposed Expectations and Grief:

Therese Rando's research explores how bereaved individuals often impose expectations upon themselves, influenced by societal norms and personal beliefs about grieving (Rando, 1993). She highlights the potential for these self-imposed expectations to complicate the grieving process and the need for self-compassion.

The Pressure to "Move On":

J. William Worden's work addresses the common expectation that the bereaved should 'move on' after a certain period, a notion that can add to the burden of grief (Worden, 2009). He advocates for a more personalized expectation of grief, where individuals can grieve at their own pace.

Resilience and Vulnerability in Grief:

Kenneth Doka and Terry Martin's studies on grieving discuss the balance between resilience and vulnerability (Doka & Martin, 2010). They examine how societal expectations often emphasize resilience at the expense of acknowledging the natural vulnerability that comes with loss.

By integrating these perspectives, this chapter explains how societal and self-imposed expectations can shape and sometimes complicate the grieving process. It offers guidance for navigating these expectations, encouraging readers to find a grief journey that is authentic.

Societal and self-imposed expectations often begin to dictate the grieving process. These insights help us understand the need for a more empathetic and individualized approach to grief that honors each person's unique experiences and allows for an authentic and self-defined expression of grief. Ultimately, this section aims to empower readers to navigate their grief journey free from the weight of unrealistic expectations, fostering a path toward healing that is both compassionate and respectful of their personal experiences of loss.

Navigating Loss: Suggestions & Support

We recognize the significant challenge of balancing societal norms, personal expectations, and the authentic expression of grief. We aim to empower you with actionable tasks that can assist in managing these pressures, allowing you to grieve in a way that is true to yourself and your unique experience. From challenging societal "rules" about grief to fostering self-compassion, the suggestions here are designed to guide you in finding a path through grief that respects your individuality and supports your healing journey. We understand that each person's experience with grief is deeply personal, and these strategies are offered to help you honor your process, free from the constraints of external and internal expectations.

Recognize and Challenge Societal Expectations: Become aware of the societal "rules" about grieving and give yourself permission to challenge them. Remember, there is no right or wrong way to grieve.

Reflect on Your Self-Imposed Expectations: Take time to reflect on any expectations you have placed on yourself and consider if they are truly serving your healing process.

Educate Yourself About Grief: Take time to educate yourself about the grieving process. There is a wide range of normal responses to loss that can empower you to embrace your unique path through grief.

Create Personal Grieving Rituals: Develop rituals that provide comfort and meaning to your grieving process. This could be anything from writing letters to your lost loved one or visiting a place with special memories.

Set Boundaries with Others: Learn to set boundaries with those who may impose their expectations on your grieving process. Politely but firmly communicate your needs and limitations when interacting with others.

Engage in Mindfulness Practices: Incorporate mindfulness practices such as meditation or mindful walking into your routine. These can help ground you in the present moment and reduce the influence of external pressures.

Journal About Your Experience: Keep a journal to document your journey through grief. Writing about your feelings can help you process them and can be a way to track your personal growth over time.

Challenge Negative Self-Talk: Be mindful of negative self-talk and challenge any critical thoughts about how you "should" be handling your grief. Replace these thoughts with kinder, more compassionate messages.

Seek Professional Help if Needed: If you find coping with societal or self-imposed expectations challenging, consider seeking help from a grief professional. Professional guidance can offer new perspectives and coping strategies.

Seek Authentic Expression: Find ways to express your authentic grief, even if it differs from what others might expect.

Build a Supportive Network: Surround yourself with people who understand and respect your individual grieving process and who offer support without expectations.

Practice Self-Compassion: Be kind to yourself, recognizing that your journey through grief is unique, and it's okay to deviate from the perceived "norm."

The journey through loss is inherently personal and often fraught with external pressures and internalized beliefs about how we "should" grieve. By embracing the suggestions outlined in this chapter, we encourage you to forge a path that honors your authentic grieving process, free from the weight of societal norms and self-imposed standards. Remember, there is no universal right way to grieve, and allowing yourself the space and permission to mourn in a way that feels right for you is crucial. May these strategies serve as a supportive guide, helping you navigate your grief with a sense of empowerment and self-compassion and, ultimately, leading you towards a healing path as an individual, as your experience of loss.

CHAPTER 19

The Fear of Forgetting: Preserving Memories

"There are places I'll remember all my life, though some have changed." —The Beatles

The fear first gripped us on a quiet evening when the world seemed to pause, and we found ourselves immersed in a photo album of Trevor. Each photograph was a gateway to the past, capturing moments of joy that once filled our lives. His smile that could light up any room, his infectious laughter, the unique quirks that made him distinctly Trevor – all were there, frozen in time. But amidst this nostalgia, a chilling thought crept uninvited into our minds: the possibility of these memories fading with time. The thought of losing the vividness of his face, the distinct timbre of his voice, and the essence of his being was terrifying. What if, as years passed, the memories we clung to for comfort began to blur? How could we ever take an intact family photo again?

This fear of forgetting, of letting slip those treasured memories, became a constant in our journey through grief. It was a haunting reminder of the fragility of memory and the relentless march of time. How could we ensure that the details of his existence and life stories didn't fade into the background of our evolving lives? The thought of being unable to recall the small things – the way his eyes crinkled when he laughed, the sound of his footsteps, and the warmth of his presence – filled us with dread.

This fear propelled us to actively find ways to keep his memory alive, not just for ourselves but for everyone he touched. It became essential to us that Trevor's legacy wasn't confined to the pages of a photo album or the recesses of our minds but continued to resonate and have a place in the world. It spurred us to create the Trevor Toes and Tushies 501(c)(3), an organization that donates new socks and underwear to kids in need, inspired by Trevor's love for wearing mismatched socks. We imagine kids who've received donations running with Trevor's energy, keeping his spirit alive.

While photographs and physical mementos are precious, preserving a memory is also about keeping their spirit alive through the stories we tell, the traditions we carry, and the legacy we build. This pursuit of memory preservation became a crucial part of our healing process, a way to honor Trevor's life and confront the fear of forgetting.

Formal family pictures without Trevor invoke such a sense of loss and sadness that we haven't been able to take traditional pictures since his passing. We tried once, hoping to include him in our family's story, and asked the photographer if Trevor could be photoshopped into the proofs. However, her response was unexpected and hurtful – she threatened to sue us if we edited her photos. This was another example of the challenges we face in a world that often doesn't comprehend the depth of our loss. Trevor's older brother, who was seven at the time of Trevor's passing, though, had an idea. He suggested we keep a stuffed penguin handy for casual family photos. Someone holds the stuffed penguin, who will forever represent Trevor. To this day, we carry a small stuffed penguin with us on vacations. It's not a perfect solution, but it's enough for our hearts not to break every time we have a photo opportunity.

This chapter emphasizes the importance of helping preserve memories for those supporting someone in grief. It discusses how friends and family can assist in creating lasting tributes and encourages sharing stories that keep the loved one's memory vibrant. The griever's desire to hold onto memories is key, as is providing supportive ways to honor and remember the lost loved one. For professionals like photographers, offering services sensitive to these needs, like photo editing to include loved ones, can be compassionate and valuable.

Her Quest for Enlightened Comprehension:

If I told you how much receiving Christmas cards hurt for years, you might find it hard to believe. Seeing a card with our individual names listed and Trevor's conspicuously absent was like a dagger to my heart, a painful reminder of his absence. Moreover, the sight of happy families boasting about their year was more than my heart could take in those early years of grief. This pain was so acute that, after Trevor passed, I decided to stop sending Christmas cards altogether. I couldn't bear the thought of inadvertently inflicting that same pain on someone else. I also secretly hoped that by not reciprocating with a card, people might eventually stop sending them to us. While the tradition of sending cards might seem like a nice gesture, it's important to consider its impact. Unless I can be confident it won't cause hurt, I believe it's safer to use a general family name or find other ways to express holiday greetings that are sensitive to everyone's circumstances.

In recent years, I've noticed we've received fewer cards. Perhaps it's because people have moved away from the tradition, or maybe it's our move to a new house, or possibly it's because I stopped sending them out. However, I must acknowledge the few people who still send cards and include Trevor's name. Their awareness and thoughtfulness in remembering him so inclusively is a loving gesture that stands out in my experience.

This change in my approach to holiday traditions reflects how grief has altered my perspective. What were once simple, joyous gestures now carry a different weight, underscoring how deeply grief can affect our actions and viewpoints. It's a poignant example of how the minutiae of life are reshaped in the wake of loss, prompting new ways of interacting with longstanding traditions.

This change in approach reflects the profound ways in which grief has altered how I view and handle what was once simple, joyous gestures. It underscores the intricate and often unexpected ways grief can change our perspectives and actions.

His Path of Insightful Realization:

The fear of forgetting – their voice, their laughter, the vitality of their presence – is a haunting reality in the aftermath of loss. As time progresses, the clarity of these memories often dims, making them more challenging to recall. This is why collecting videos and pictures becomes so crucial. I've realized the importance of keeping these treasures in a place where they are easily accessible, allowing me to revisit those cherished moments whenever the fear of forgetting creeps in.

The cessation of time at the moment of death brings with it a unique sorrow, especially when it comes to the loss of a child. Trevor will forever be six years old in my memories. There's a deep sadness in not knowing what he would have grown up to be. It's hard to picture him as a teenager, to imagine the paths he might have chosen, the career he could have pursued. The natural curiosity about the mistakes he would have made, the lessons he would have learned, and the person he would have become remains unanswered.

To counter this, I've found solace in creating a collection of items that evoke his essence, that bring his existence momentarily back to life in my heart and mind. This collection is more than just a set of objects; it's a tangible connection to Trevor. Pictures that capture his brightest moments, movies that echo his laughter, toys that were once his prized possessions, his favorite things, the foods he loved, places we visited together, activities we enjoyed – each holds a fragment of his story. They serve as a bridge between the past and present, allowing me to connect with him and keep his memory vibrant and alive.

Collecting and preserving memories is a way of honoring Trevor and confronting the fear of forgetting. It's a testament to his impact on our lives, ensuring that his spirit continues to be integral to our family's narrative while he may not be physically present.

Research Perspectives:

There is a therapeutic role of recollecting and cherishing memories. These experts in grief and bereavement help us understand the psychological importance of remembering our loved ones. The goal is to offer insights that resonate with the personal experiences of those navigating the delicate journey of remembering while grieving.

The Psychological Importance of Memory Preservation:

Colin Murray Parkes' research has illuminated the psychological importance of preserving memories after a loss (Parkes, 1972). He discusses how tangible reminders, such as photographs and mementos, can be important links to the loved one, aiding the grieving process.

Memory and Continuing Bonds:

Therese Rando has explored how maintaining a connection with the loved one through memories can be a crucial part of the grieving process (Rando, 1993). She emphasizes that preserving memories can help continue the bond with the loved one, a key aspect of adapting to loss.

Narrative and Memory in Grief:

J. William Worden's work includes the concept of narrative and memory in grief (Worden, 2009). He suggests that recounting stories and memories of the loved one can be a therapeutic part of the mourning process, helping to keep the memory of the loved one alive.

Tangible Memorials and Grieving:

Kenneth Doka and Terry Martin's studies have shown that creating tangible memorials, such as memory boxes or dedicated spaces, can be a meaningful way to preserve the memories of the loved one (Doka & Martin, 2010). These memorials can offer a sense of closeness to the loved one and comfort the bereaved.

By integrating these research perspectives, this chapter offers insights into the vital role of preserving memories in the grieving process. The therapeutic value of holding onto memories and creating memorials is significant. It emphasizes that while our loved ones may no longer be physically present, their memories can continue to live on through our efforts to preserve and honor them. Ultimately, this section serves as a valuable resource for readers seeking to navigate the fear of forgetting, guiding how to cherish and maintain the legacy of those who have passed away.

Navigating Loss: Suggestions & Support

Here, we offer a range of creative and meaningful suggestions to help you maintain a connection with your loved one and cherish the memories you hold dear. From tangible projects like creating memory boxes or albums to more intangible acts like continuing traditions or sharing stories, these strategies are designed to support you in commemorating your loved one in a way that feels personal and significant. Our goal is to provide you with ideas that not only help preserve the memories of your loved one but also offer comfort and a sense of ongoing connection during your journey through grief.

Create Memory Boxes or Albums: Compile photos, letters, and mementos into a special box or album as a tangible remembrance of your loved one.

Write or Record Your Memories: Journal your thoughts and memories or record them as audio or video. This can be a personal way to preserve your recollections.

Design a Memory Corner: Set up a dedicated space in your home, like a memory corner, where you can display items that remind you of your loved one. This can include photographs, their favorite books, or even a piece of clothing they loved.

Create a Memory Playlist: Compile a playlist of songs that remind you of your loved one or were their favorites. Music can be a powerful trigger for memories and emotions.

Start a Memory Blog or Website: Create a blog or a website where you can share stories, photos, and memories of your loved one. This can also be a platform for friends and family to share memories.

Craft a Memory Quilt or Artwork: If you're crafty, consider making a quilt or artwork using materials that remind you of your loved one, such as pieces of their clothing or items they cherished.

Celebrate Their Favorite Traditions: Continue to celebrate traditions important to your loved one, whether making their favorite meal on their birthday or watching their favorite movie on special occasions.

Write Letters to Your Loved One: Write letters to your loved one on significant dates or whenever you need to connect with them. This can be a cathartic way to express your feelings and keep their memory alive.

Include Them in Family Conversations: Keep your loved one's memory alive by including them in family conversations. Talk about what they would have thought or said in certain situations, or reminisce about happy times spent together.

Organize Memorial Events: Consider organizing events on significant dates that celebrate the life and legacy of your loved one, keeping their memory alive within your community.

Share Stories: Share stories about your loved one with others. This not only helps preserve their memory but can also provide comfort.

Engage in Legacy Projects: Engage in projects or activities that reflect the interests or values of your loved one, such as charity work or creative endeavors.

Create a Living Memorial: Plant a garden tree or create a space in your home that serves as a living tribute to your loved one.

We understand that each memory holds a special place in your heart, and preserving these memories is vital to the grieving process. The suggestions in this chapter are intended to give you various options for honoring and remembering your loved one, from physical memorials to expressive and creative acts. Remember, there is no right or wrong way to preserve memories; what matters most is finding a method that resonates with you and reflects your unique relationship with your loved one. May these suggestions serve as a guiding light in your journey of remembrance, helping you to find solace and connection as you cherish the legacy of the person you hold dear.

CHAPTER 20

Faith and Spirituality: Navigating the Spiritual Landscape

"What we have once enjoyed and deeply loved we can never lose, for all that we love deeply becomes part of us."
—Helen Keller

Shortly after Trevor passed, we had the opportunity to visit a psychic medium. We were skeptical, but a part of us needed to see it through to understand how this scenario would play out. In our session, we heard details about Trevor's final morning – details no one could have known. The level of detail the medium knew and shared lessened our skepticism. We recognize this isn't a path for everyone and respect that; truthfully, it wasn't a path for us until our longing to hear from Trevor grew too intense to ignore. We are grateful for people with these gifts, for offering a form of connection that, in our grief, we so desperately sought.

For many, like myself, loss can lead to profound questioning and reevaluation of spiritual beliefs. This section offers insights for those grappling with spiritual doubts, guiding them in exploring these questions and finding personal meaning in the midst of sorrow. It's about acknowledging that faith can be challenged and strengthened in the face of grief and that each journey through these spiritual questions is deeply personal.

For supporters, this chapter underscores the importance of offering compassionate, non-judgmental support to those navigating changes in their spiritual beliefs. It's about respecting that everyone's spiritual journey in grief is unique and respecting the individual's process of seeking meaning and purpose. This part of the chapter offers perspectives on how to be a source of comfort without imposing one's own beliefs or expectations. It's a reminder that spiritual journeys can take many forms, and what brings to one person may differ from another. The role of a supporter is to be a steadfast presence, offering empathy and an open heart to the myriad ways people find hope and connection in their spiritual explorations.

Her Quest for Enlightened Comprehension:

Seven years had passed since we lost Trevor when we decided to move out of the house where we had lived during his time with us. As I stood in the center of our new living room, Trevor's ashes settled in the same cabinet they had occupied in our old home, and a wave of complex emotions washed over me. This new space was markedly different, yet there were elements, little "Trevor" aspects, that we had intentionally brought with us. These items served as bridges between our past with Trevor and our present without him.

In this new environment, devoid of direct memories of Trevor, I surprisingly found his presence to be palpable. His spirit had accompanied us, transcending the physical spaces where our memories were made. I searched my heart and mind for signs that had become synonymous with Trevor. The appearance of a white feather would bring a sense of closeness, a symbolic reminder of him. Spotting a hawk soaring effortlessly on the wind, not flapping its wings but gliding with grace, evoked a feeling of connection to Trevor as if he were still with us in some form.

Whenever a Michael Jackson song, one of Trevor's favorites, played unexpectedly, it felt like a small nod from the universe, a gentle reminder of his enduring presence in our lives, and a flash, I can hear and see him singing "Beat It." These moments, these signs, became my way of keeping Trevor's memory alive, a means of feeling his presence in a home that he had never physically inhabited. They were more than coincidences; they were comforting affirmations that Trevor's spirit was still intertwined with our own, manifesting in subtle yet profoundly meaningful ways.

This new home, while lacking the direct memories of Trevor, became a place where I could feel his essence. It was a testament that the bonds of love and remembrance are not confined to physical spaces but continue to live in the hearts of those who cherish them. These small yet significant connections to Trevor provided a sense of continuity, a bridge between the past and the present, and a comforting assurance that although he was not with us in body, his spirit remained an integral part of our family and our new home.

His Path of Insightful Realization:

The belief in an afterlife has been a source of immense comfort to me, especially in navigating the loss of Trevor. It's a conviction beyond mere hope; it's a deep-seated faith that Trevor's spirit is still around, not just with me but with the loved ones we've both lost. This belief gives me a sense of continuity, a feeling that our connection didn't cease with his physical departure from this world.

I often find solace in the thought that one day, when my journey in this life concludes, I will be reunited with Trevor. This faith in an afterlife provides a sense of anticipation for a future reunion, allowing me to view Trevor's death not as an end but as a pause in our relationship. It's a comforting thought that there's more to our story, that the chapters of our time together are yet to be completed.

This belief allows me to perceive our relationship as temporarily on hold rather than permanently severed. It enables me to talk to Trevor in spirit, to share my thoughts and feelings with him as if he's still a part of my everyday life. While I know I won't receive responses as I used to, there's a profound comfort in simply speaking to him, in keeping the lines of communication open in my heart and mind.

In moments of solitude, I often speak to Trevor, sharing updates about our lives, expressing my love, and sometimes, just recounting memories. It's a practice that keeps his memory vivid and alive in my heart. This ongoing conversation, though one-sided in the physical sense, feels deeply reciprocal in a spiritual sense. It's as if by keeping Trevor in my thoughts and speaking to him, I'm maintaining the bond we shared, bridging the gap between the physical and the spiritual realms.

This faith in the afterlife and the continuation of our bond has been a source of comfort and a guiding force in my life. It reminds me to cherish my relationships, live a life that honors Trevor's memory, and embrace the belief that death is not the final goodbye but rather a temporary parting until we meet again.

Research Perspectives:

We investigate how individuals turn to faith and spiritual practices to find solace and meaning in the face of loss. This section offers a diverse range of perspectives, examining how different faiths and belief systems approach the concepts of grief and mourning and how these beliefs can both challenge and comfort those grieving. Our objective is to provide readers with a comprehensive understanding of how faith and spirituality can influence and support the grieving process, offering insights and guidance for those navigating their spiritual journey in the wake of loss.

The Role of Faith in Grieving:

Elisabeth Kübler-Ross, in her seminal work on death and dying, discusses how faith can play a crucial role in grieving (Kübler-Ross, 1969). She explains that faith can offer solace and a framework for understanding the loss, helping individuals find meaning in their experiences.

Spirituality and the Search for Meaning:

Working alongside Kübler-Ross, David Kessler extends this discussion by exploring how spirituality often leads to a search for meaning in the wake of loss (Kessler, 2019). He suggests that engaging with spiritual practices can provide a sense of purpose and connection in grief.

Grief and Religious Coping:

Kenneth Pargament has extensively researched the concept of religious coping and how individuals use their faith and religious beliefs to handle stress and grief (Pargament, 1997). His studies indicate that positive religious coping can lead to better psychological adjustment in bereavement.

Interfaith Perspectives on Grief:

Harold Koenig's work provides an interfaith perspective on grief, examining how different religious traditions approach loss and mourning (Koenig, 2007). He highlights the diversity in grieving practices and the importance of respecting individual spiritual paths in the grieving process.

Spirituality can provide a framework for understanding loss, a source of comfort in times of despair, and a pathway to finding meaning and purpose after a loved one's passing. Here, we emphasize the diversity of spiritual responses to grief and the importance of respecting and supporting each individual's unique spiritual journey. Ultimately, this section serves as a resource for those seeking to understand the spiritual dimensions of their grief, providing guidance and reassurance that faith and spirituality can be a source of strength and solace in the difficult journey of mourning.

Navigating Loss: Suggestions & Support

Recognizing that the journey through grief often brings profound spiritual questions and challenges, this section offers a variety of strategies to help you navigate these complex aspects. Whether you seek to reaffirm your faith, explore new spiritual paths, or find solace in spiritual practices, the suggestions here are designed to support and guide you. Our goal is to offer a compassionate and respectful approach to exploring faith and spirituality, providing you with tools and resources to help you find a sense of peace and understanding on your journey through grief.

Explore Your Spiritual Questions: Give yourself permission to question and explore your spiritual beliefs. This exploration can be an important part of your healing process.

Meditation and Mindfulness Practices: Engage in meditation or mindfulness practices. These can help you find inner peace and be a way to feel connected to your loved one or a higher power.

Read Inspirational Literature: Explore books, poems, or scriptures that offer comfort or insight into your spiritual questions. Reading can provide solace and a different perspective on your experience.

Attend Spiritual Workshops or Retreats: Consider attending workshops or retreats focusing on spirituality and grief. These can be spaces for healing and connecting with others on a similar journey.

Reflect on Memories in a Spiritual Context: Reflect on your memories with your loved one in the context of your spiritual beliefs. This can be a way to find meaning and comfort in those shared moments.

Volunteer or Engage in Charitable Work: Volunteering or engaging in charitable work can be a way to honor your loved one's memory and can provide a sense of purpose and fulfillment.

Create a Spiritual Space in Your Home: Design a space dedicated to spiritual reflection, meditation, or remembering your loved one. This can be a sanctuary to connect with your spirituality and memories.

Express Your Spirituality Creatively: If you are artistically inclined, express your spirituality and memories through creative means such as painting, writing, music, or crafting.

Seek Supportive Communities: Engage with spiritual or religious communities that resonate with your current beliefs and feelings, or find support groups that focus on spirituality in grief.

Incorporate Rituals and Practices: Consider incorporating rituals or practices that bring comfort or connect you with your loved one, whether traditional religious practices or more personal, spiritual expressions.

Journal Your Spiritual Journey: Keep a journal to document your thoughts, feelings, and questions about faith and spirituality. Writing can be a powerful tool for processing your spiritual journey.

Connect with Nature or Art: Sometimes, spirituality can be found in nature or through creative expression. Spend time in natural settings or engage in artistic activities that provide a sense of peace and connection.

Seek Spiritual Counseling: If you are struggling with your faith or spirituality, consider seeking guidance from a spiritual leader or professional who can provide support and perspective.

Spirituality and faith can play a significant role in the grieving process. We encourage you to try a few of the strategies mentioned as a means to explore and affirm your faith and spirituality in a way that is meaningful and comforting to you. May this journey through faith and spirituality bring you a sense of hope and some comfort.

CHAPTER 21

The Lingering Questions: Finding Answers and Acceptance in Our Journey

"The art of living lies less in eliminating our troubles than in growing with them." —Bernard M. Baruch

Trevor's actual cause of death remains unknown. A perfectly healthy child was tucked into bed, and in the early morning hours, during his sleep, his time on earth abruptly ended. Despite numerous autopsies, none could provide an answer. It's called "Sudden Unexplained Death in Childhood" (SUDC). This is a reality we will never stop wondering about. The lack of answers places us in a precarious position whenever we have to make medical decisions for Trevor's siblings. It's also been something difficult to accept. There are times when we find ourselves feeling a sense of jealousy toward other grieving families who know the cause of their loved one's death. Then, our rational mind steps in, reminding us that death is still death and that even with a known cause, there are always unknowns, such as what precisely led to the final moment. Knowing the cause certainly doesn't diminish the pain of loss.

In this chapter, we offer insights to those who repeatedly revisit unanswered questions, seeking meaning in the seemingly senseless nature of grief. It's crucial to recognize that, while some questions may forever remain unanswered, there is a path toward acceptance and finding peace amidst this uncertainty. We delve into the significance of self-compassion as a crucial element in this quest for answers. Furthermore, we emphasize the importance of creating a non-judgmental space for those providing support, where grieving individuals can openly express their lingering questions. These questions are a natural aspect of the grieving process, and offering empathy rather than immediate solutions is paramount. Fostering open, honest communication that validates the importance of the griever's quest for answers can be a significant source of comfort for those in grief. This chapter is about navigating through the complexities of unanswered questions and finding a way to live with the unknown, integrating it into our journey of grief and acceptance.

Her Quest for Enlightened Comprehension:

Navigating acceptance has, for me, been one of the most challenging aspects of this journey. Even nine years after Trevor's passing, a part of me still grapples with the finality of his absence. Sometimes, in quiet moments or distractions, I still half-expect him to walk through the front door. When this happens, my heart momentarily leaps with an impossible hope before reality sets back in with a jolt of sadness. This reaction, this fleeting surge of excitement, is quickly followed by that familiar catch in my throat – a sharp reminder that he is truly gone.

Coming to terms with Trevor's absence has been a gradual journey marked by small moments of realization and acceptance. The initial years were the hardest, with every reminder of Trevor bringing profound shock and disbelief. It felt as if my heart and mind were in constant conflict, my emotions unwilling to accept what my intellect knew to be true.

As the years have passed, I've noticed a subtle shift in how I react to these moments. The sharpness of surprise and disbelief has slowly softened. When I experience that brief catch in my throat, it's no longer a prolonged struggle. The shock dissipates more quickly, giving way to a quiet acceptance. It's a testament to the slow but relentless passage of time and the gradual healing of grief.

This acceptance doesn't mean I've forgotten Trevor or that the pain of his loss has disappeared. It means I've learned to live with the reality of his absence in a way that allows me to remember him with more love than pain. It's a form of reconciliation with the loss – an understanding that Trevor's presence has shifted from a physical reality to an enduring memory in our hearts. The process of reaching this point of acceptance has been long and often painful, but it represents a significant milestone in my journey through grief. It's a bittersweet acknowledgment that life goes on, albeit with Trevor forever in our hearts.

His Path of Insightful Realization:

As time has passed since Trevor's death, I've come to understand the adage "Time heals all wounds" in a more profound sense. In the immediate aftermath of our loss, the notion that time could bring healing seemed almost inconceivable. Yet, as significant milestones and anniversaries have come and gone, I've noticed a gradual shift in my perspective. With each passing year, the raw intensity of grief has found a more settled place in my heart, leading to a form of acceptance.

This journey towards acceptance hasn't been about finding clear answers to the painful questions that loss brings. Instead, it's been a process of learning to live with these questions, to find peace in the uncertainty and the unknown. The realization that our time on earth is finite and unpredictable has, in a way, brought a measure of comfort. It's a stark reminder of the fragile nature of life and the inevitability of death for all of us.

In facing the reality of death, I've found solace in my faith and the belief in an afterlife. This belief has been a cornerstone of my journey through grief, providing a sense of continuity beyond the physical world. The thought that my spirit will one day reunite with Trevor and those who have passed before me offers a sense of hope amidst the finality of death. It's a comforting thought that our separation is temporary and that there is a spiritual continuation where we will be together again.

Time's relentless march forward has been a catalyst for this acceptance. It's taught me that healing isn't about eradicating the pain of loss but about integrating this experience into the fabric of life. Acceptance doesn't mean forgetting or moving on from the memory of Trevor. Instead, it means acknowledging that our time together was precious and finite. My connection to him now exists in a different realm – memory, legacy, and spiritual belief. In this way, time has played a crucial role in soothing the wounds of grief, guiding me toward a place of peace and acceptance.

Research Perspectives:

While grief is deeply personal and unique to each individual, the insights gained from rigorous research can provide valuable signposts along the journey. We explore the latest findings, evidence-based strategies, and expert perspectives to shed light on the profound complexities of grief, offering you a compass to navigate the uncharted territory of loss. These research insights serve as beacons of hope, helping you find your way through the darkest moments of grief toward a path of healing and acceptance.

The Nature of Grieving and Unanswered Questions:

Elisabeth Kübler-Ross's groundbreaking work on the stages of grief provides a foundation for understanding how unanswered questions are a natural part of the grieving process (Kübler-Ross, 1969). She emphasizes that seeking answers is a common way individuals try to make sense of their loss. The stages of grief are not sequential steps but rather a spectrum of emotions that one might navigate in varying order and intensity during the grieving process, highlighting the diverse and individual nature of coping with loss.

The Concept of "Continuing Bonds":

Therese Rando's research introduces the concept of "continuing bonds," which can help individuals find acceptance in their grief journey (Rando, 1993). She suggests that maintaining a connection with the loved one can be a meaningful way to navigate the pain and uncertainty of loss.

Time and the Healing Process:

J. William Worden's work on grief counseling highlights the role of time in the healing process (Worden, 2009). He discusses how time, while not erasing grief, can help individuals find a new sense of normalcy and acceptance.

Cognitive Approaches to Grieving:

Robert Neimeyer's focus on the cognitive aspects of grieving sheds light on how constructing a narrative can aid in answering some of the lingering questions (Neimeyer, 2006). He explores how storytelling and meaning-making are crucial in the journey towards acceptance.

Fostering Acceptance:

Acceptance and Commitment Therapy (ACT) encourages acceptance of emotional pain, which is particularly relevant for individuals facing unresolved aspects of grief. It helps acknowledge the loss's reality and the accompanying unanswered questions without getting entangled in "why" or "what if" scenarios (Hayes & Wilson, 2021). According to Hayes and Wilson, ACT focuses on helping individuals accept their reactions and be present with what life brings without unnecessary struggle. This approach especially benefits those grappling with the unknowns in their grief journey. ACT teaches that while we cannot always control or change external events or the past, we can learn to accept our reactions and work towards living a value-driven life. In the case of unresolved grief, this means acknowledging the pain and uncertainty while continuing to engage in life in a meaningful way.

By incorporating these diverse perspectives, this chapter offers a comprehensive understanding of how grief is navigated through unanswered questions and the search for acceptance. It guides those seeking to reconcile with their loss and find a sense of peace.

Navigating Loss: Suggestions & Support

Grief is not a linear journey with a neatly defined endpoint. Instead, it can be a labyrinth of uncertainty, where questions and doubts are as much a part of the terrain as sorrow and acceptance. Through expert insights and personal experiences, we aim to provide solace and guidance to those traversing this intricate landscape.

Reflect on Your Questions: Allow yourself to reflect on the questions that arise, recognizing them as a normal part of grieving. Writing them down can be a therapeutic way to process these thoughts.

Engage in Conversations: Discuss your questions with trusted friends, family members, or support groups. Sometimes, speaking aloud can provide a new perspective or offer relief.

Seek Professional Guidance: If you struggle with these questions, consider seeking guidance from a grief professional. Professional support can offer new insights and coping strategies.

Set Aside Time for Mindful Moments: Choose a regular time each day to practice mindfulness. This could be a few minutes in the morning, during a break in your day, or in the evening.

Focus on the Present Moment: Begin by focusing on your breath, noticing the sensation of air entering and leaving your body. Observe your thoughts and feelings without judgment, allowing them to come and go.

Engage in Mindful Activities: Incorporate mindfulness into daily activities. This could be as simple as paying full attention to the process of making a cup of tea, taking a mindful walk where you consciously notice your surroundings, or eating a meal with full awareness of the flavors and textures.

Practice Acceptance: When challenging thoughts or emotions arise, acknowledge them. Remember that having these thoughts and feelings is okay and doesn't define you. Allow them to be present without trying to change or resist them.

Reflect on Your Values: Spend time reflecting on what is truly important to you – your values. This could involve writing down your values and considering how your daily actions can align more closely with these values. Make a conscious effort each day to take small steps that align with your values, whether nurturing relationships, engaging in work or hobbies that are meaningful to you, or taking care of your health and well-being. This approach fosters a compassionate acceptance of your emotional landscape while encouraging you to live a life that reflects your values and aspirations.

Explore Different Philosophies and Beliefs: Delve into different philosophies, spiritual beliefs, or literature that might offer different perspectives on life, loss, and the meaning of suffering.

Practice Mindfulness and Meditation: Engage in mindfulness or meditation to find peace in the present moment. This can help in accepting the unknown and finding tranquility amidst the questions.

Create a Ritual to Honor Your Questions: Consider creating a personal ritual to honor and acknowledge your questions, like lighting a candle or writing a letter. This can be a way of making peace with the uncertainties.

As we conclude our exploration of the lingering questions that accompany grief, we want you to know that you are not alone in your quest for answers and acceptance. Grief is a journey that unfolds at its own pace, and while questions may persist, they need not overshadow the memories and love you hold for your lost loved one. In seeking answers, you are engaging in a profound act of remembrance and honoring the significance of what has been lost. As you continue your journey, may you find the peace and acceptance you seek, and may your loved one's memory shine as a beacon of love and connection in the depths of your heart.

CHAPTER 22

Transformative Energies of Grief and Unexpected Blessings Found Along the Way

"Grief, I've learned, is really just love.
It's all the love you want to give, but cannot. All that
unspent love gathers up in the corners of your eyes, the lump
in your throat, and in that hollow part of your chest. Grief
is just love with no place to go." —Jamie Anderson

O ther unexpected blessings include newfound empathy and a deepened capacity for compassion towards others who are suffering. Through our journey of grief, we've become acutely aware of the struggles others face, creating a sense of solidarity with those in pain. We've also found an increased appreciation for life's preciousness and a renewed focus on what truly matters. This shift in perspective has led us to cherish small moments and prioritize relationships over material possessions. Moreover, the intense energy of grief has sometimes sparked a creative awakening, where expressing our emotions through art, writing, or music has become a therapeutic outlet and a way to honor our lost loved ones.

Grief is an intense energy, a powerful force that engulfs us. It's both debilitating and strangely invigorating. In the throes of loss, we often find ourselves experiencing a heightened sense of awareness, a deeper connection to our emotions, and an unfiltered view of life. This raw energy, if harnessed, can be transformative. It's akin to a raging river. Uncontrolled, it can devastate everything in its path. But when channeled, it can generate immense power. In grief coaching, many have redirected this energy into creative pursuits, community service, or deeper personal development, turning their pain into a force for positive change.

Finding gifts in loss may seem paradoxical, but it's a profound truth for many. Loss teaches us about resilience, the depths of love, and the importance of connections. It can strip away life's superficialities, leaving a raw yet more authentic existence. In our moments of deepest despair, we often uncover parts of ourselves we never knew existed. Strength we never knew we had. Compassion we never fully expressed. These are the unexpected blessings of grief – they don't negate the pain but coexist with it, offering a glimmer of hope in the darkness. These transformative energies, often unrecognized at first, gradually reveal themselves, helping us find meaning and moments of joy amidst the sorrow.

Her Quest for Enlightened Comprehension:

The most profound gifts I've received from my loss, held dearly in my heart, are centered on a life-altering realization: life can shift in a moment. This insight, born from the depths of my grief, has profoundly reshaped my approach to life. I now live daily with deliberate intention and purpose, embracing experiences, relationships, and moments with a newfound passion and intensity. Adopting a life without regrets as a guiding principle, I've become deeply conscious of time's transience.

This awareness drives me to make choices that align with my true self and deepest values. I now take risks more freely, express love without hesitation, and pursue activities that bring me true joy and fulfillment.

This transformation extends beyond my journey; it has fundamentally changed how I connect with others. Empathy and being present have become the cornerstones of my relationships. I've also embraced a profound sense of purpose in supporting others navigating grief, recognizing the importance of this role.

The quality and depth of my connections have become paramount. I treasure meaningful interactions, valuing the authenticity and depth they add to my life. Therefore, the most significant gifts from my loss transcend personal change. They represent a deeper engagement with the world around me. I've learned to savor the beauty of the present, the value of genuine relationships, and the importance of living a life that reflects my true desires and beliefs. In this way, my loss has been a catalyst for a richer, more purposeful existence.

His Path of Insightful Realization:

As an experience, grief often acts as a unifying force, drawing people together under its encompassing canopy. When Trevor passed away, I found myself unexpectedly initiated into a fellowship no one willingly joins, yet within which everyone finds a sense of belonging. This unique community is bonded not by choice but by the shared heartache of loss. It's a bond that brings people from all walks of life to a common ground of empathy.

Conversations about our children are not just normal but necessary in this space. They're a vital part of the healing process. We talk about our lost children, their lives, their quirks, our memories with them, and the void they've left behind. This shared narrative creates an immediate and deeply comforting connection. It's a connection that starts from a place of shared pain, where everyone understands the gravity of each other's loss without needing it to be explained.

The loss of a child also prompts a deep introspection about our roles as parents. It forces us to reevaluate our parenting styles, relationships with our surviving children, and perceptions of being a parent. For me, it led to a redefinition of my parenting approach. The traditional paths no longer seemed adequate or relevant. Instead, I adopted a style that aligned more closely with my "new normal" – a life reshaped by loss and the lessons it imparts.

This shift in parenting style may not always be understood or accepted by others. It's a byproduct of child loss that many of us in this group have come to accept. Our perspectives on life, parenting, and relationships have been irrevocably altered. We find solace within our group, where such changes are acknowledged and embraced as part of the complex grief journey.

Thus, in the aftermath of such profound loss, we find ourselves evolving in our identities and roles as parents and community members. This evolution is not easy and is often misunderstood by those outside our circle, but within the group, it's a shared and accepted part of our collective journey through grief.

Research Perspectives:

The insights from various experts offer a deeper comprehension of the grieving process, illuminating how it can be both a journey of profound sorrow and unexpected transformation. The goal of this section is not only to provide theoretical perspectives but also to connect with and support those navigating the intricate pathways of grief. By delving into these research perspectives, readers are invited to find solace in knowing their experiences are unique and universally shared.

Kübler-Ross and Kessler (2005) highlight the non-linear progression of grief, emphasizing that the well-known stages – denial, anger, bargaining, depression, and acceptance – are not steps to be checked off but emotions to be experienced (Kübler-Ross & Kessler, 2005). This perspective helps validate individuals' varied emotional responses to loss.

Worden's (2009) task-based model for mourning emphasizes the active work of grieving, proposing four tasks that must be undertaken for healing: accepting the reality of the loss, processing the pain of grief, adjusting to a world without the loved one, and finding an enduring connection with the loved one while embarking on a new life (Worden, 2009). This model provides a framework for understanding the complexities of adapting to loss.

Stroebe and Schut's (1999) Dual Process Model of Coping with Bereavement offers a dynamic view of grieving, alternating between loss-oriented and restoration-oriented activities (Stroebe & Schut, 1999). Their research suggests that a healthy grieving process involves oscillating between confronting and avoiding the realities of loss, thus giving individuals a more flexible approach to coping with their grief.

Lastly, Neimeyer's (2001) work on the significance of meaning-making in the grieving process sheds light on how constructing a narrative around loss can aid healing (Neimeyer, 2001). This perspective emphasizes the importance of personal stories and experiences in navigating the journey of grief.

The journey through grief, as depicted by these research perspectives, is a complex and deeply personal experience. However, it's important to remember that each person's journey is unique. These theories are not prescriptions but guides to help navigate the turbulent waters of loss. As we close this section, we hope these research perspectives provide comfort and a sense of connection for those on the often lonely road of grief. Remember, in the midst of loss, there is also the potential for profound growth and unexpected blessings.

Navigating Loss: Suggestions & Support

As you navigate the complex and deeply personal journey of grief, it is important to remember that you are not alone. Here, we offer practical, compassionate guidance tailored to assist you through the transformative energies of grief and the unexpected blessings that may emerge. The tasks and suggestions are rooted in empathy, aiming to support your healing process. Each step, while small, is a vital part of your journey towards reconciliation with your loss and rediscovery of joy and meaning in life.

Embrace Your Emotions: Allow yourself to experience the full range of emotions that come with grief. Remember, it's normal to feel denial, anger, bargaining, depression, and acceptance at different times. There is no right or wrong way to feel.

Create a Memory Journal: Start a journal dedicated to your lost loved one. Write down memories, stories, and feelings associated with them. This can be a powerful way to process your grief and keep their memory alive.

Set Small, Daily Goals: Focus on setting small, achievable goals daily. These could be as simple as going for a short walk, calling a friend, or reading a book. This helps bring structure and a sense of accomplishment to your days.

Practice Self-Compassion: Be gentle with yourself. Grieving is complicated, and giving yourself grace and self-compassion is essential.

Explore Creative Outlets: Engage in creative activities such as painting, writing, or gardening. These activities can be therapeutic and provide a healthy outlet for expressing emotions.

Seek Supportive Connections: Spend time with people who understand and support your grieving process. This could be friends, family, or a support group for those who have experienced similar losses.

Reflect on Your Parenting Style: If applicable, take time to reflect on how your loss has affected your approach to parenting. Consider what changes you might want to make to align with your new perspective on life.

Engage in Meaningful Rituals: Create rituals that honor the memory of your loved one. This could be visiting their grave, lighting a candle, or celebrating their birthday in a special way.

Focus on the Present Moment: Practice mindfulness and try to stay present. This can help reduce feelings of overwhelm and keep you grounded.

Plan for Triggering Moments: Be aware of dates, places, or events that might trigger your grief. Plan ahead for how you will manage these moments, whether seeking extra support or engaging in self-care activities.

The path through grief is unique for each individual, and the suggestions provided here are intended as gentle guideposts to help you find your way. Remember, healing is not linear, and moving at your own pace is okay. These tasks empower you, offering strategies to cope, reflect, and eventually find a sense of peace and renewed purpose. As you continue on your journey, know that it's normal to have both setbacks and breakthroughs. Be kind to yourself, and allow these suggestions to be a source of support and comfort as you navigate the complexities of grief and its transformative experiences.

CHAPTER 23

The Beacon of Hope: Navigating Forward

"We must accept finite disappointment,
but never lose infinite hope." —Martin Luther King Jr.

I n the labyrinth of grief, where shadows of loss loom large, and the path ahead seems shrouded in uncertainty, hope emerges as a beacon, guiding us toward healing. This chapter is dedicated to exploring the transformative power of hope in the journey of grief. Here, we delve into the profound wisdom gleaned from various sources that illuminate the role of hope in overcoming sorrow. We examine how hope, in its many forms, acts as a vital force, not just a distant light at the end of a tunnel, but a constant companion that helps us navigate each step in the present. We aim to offer a compass that allows for patience and grace that helps through the grieving process, affirming that even amidst the deepest despair, the seeds of hope can be found and nurtured to bloom once again.

Her Quest for Enlightened Comprehension:

In this tumultuous sea of grief, where my emotions ebb and flow with conflicting desires and painful memories, I find myself grappling with the concept of hope. In my current state, hope may not yet manifest as a clear vision of a brighter future or a confident stride toward healing. Instead, it appears more subtly intertwined with my daily struggles. It's present in those brief moments when I acknowledge my loss openly, yet also when I yearn for solitude. It's hidden in my mixed feelings about social interactions – the simultaneous need for inclusion and the overwhelming desire for retreat.

Hope, for me, is also in recognizing that my complicated needs are part of grieving. It's in the gradual acceptance that my reactions, however conflicting they may seem, are part of a natural response to an unimaginable loss. This form of hope might not provide immediate solace or answers. Still, it offers a small yet significant comfort – the knowledge that my feelings are shared by others who have experienced similar losses and that these feelings are valid and understood.

In this new life, where happiness seems overshadowed by the absence of Trevor, hope is the gentle reminder that this intensity of grief will not always be as overpowering. It lies in the potential for future moments where memories bring smiles alongside tears, where mentions of Trevor evoke a smile and sadness, and that I will get better at holding both simultaneously. It's the hope that, in time, I will always honor his memory in a way that feels right for me and, in doing so, keep his spirit alive.

Hope, then, becomes less about a return to my former life of ease and more about finding a path forward where Trevor's memory continues to be a part of me. It's about learning to carry my love for him into the future, allowing it to shape me in new, meaningful ways. This hope doesn't diminish the reality of my loss, but it offers a lens through which I can view my grief – not as an impossible barrier to happiness, but as a profound part of my life's journey, marked by love as much as by loss.

In this perspective, hope is not a quick fix or an escape from grief but a companion on your journey, evolving and adapting as you navigate through your loss. It offers a way to view your experience through a lens of gradual healing and personal growth.

His Path of Insightful Realization:

On this journey of grief, hope has manifested in various forms since Trevor's passing, each phase reflecting a different aspect of my healing process. Initially, hope took the shape of denial – a yearning for the unimaginable reality that this was merely a bad dream and I would awaken to find my family whole again, with everything as it should be. However, as the stark reality set in, my concept of hope evolved. It transformed into a longing for acceptance and a belief in life everlasting, a comforting thought that one day I would reunite with Trevor in another realm when my time in this life concludes.

As time progressed, hope began to appear in more everyday moments. I hoped someone would ask about Trevor, allowing me to remember him aloud and share his memory with others. This form of hope was a bridge to keeping his spirit alive, allowing me to feel connected to him through stories and shared memories. Hope also emerged as a forward-looking sentiment, a beacon guiding me toward a future with the potential for better and happier days.

One of my more persistent hopes has been the desire to retain the vividness of Trevor's memory – the sound of his voice, the image of his smile. I've realized, though, that this aspect of hope is less about fear of forgetting and more about the constant presence of his memory in my daily life. Trevor's spirit and stories are always ready in my mind, a testament to the enduring nature of love and memory.

Navigating grief through holidays, birthdays, and school years has shifted my perception of time – from counting down to something to marking the time since Trevor's passing. Yet, hope has been a crucial ally in these moments, helping me find ways to honor Trevor's memory and embrace the future.

In the context of loss, hope is not just about coping with absence; it's about finding ways to integrate that loss into life's tapestry. It's about recognizing that life still holds spaces for joy and new beginnings, even after such profound change. Hope is the thread that weaves through the fabric of grief, reminding us that while life may be irrevocably altered, it continues to offer opportunities for growth, love, and happiness.

Research Perspectives:

Hope and grief, grief and hope... It's essential to understand the intricate relationship between these two emotions. Hope, often found within the heart of grief, is not about denying the pain or loss. It is not toxic positivity. Hope is the belief that a thriving future is possible and that you have the power to make it so, despite the present challenges! Embracing grief and hope is crucial for emotional healing and growth, as hope counterbalances the heaviness of grief.

However, transitioning to a state of hope is not immediate, especially after a loss. Casey Gwinn, J.D., and Chan Hellman, Ph.D., discuss the "survival window" following a loss, a period characterized by intense emotional turmoil, including feelings like despair, rage, or fear (Gwinn & Hellman, 2022). This phase is critical, laying the groundwork for future hope and challenging it significantly. Recognizing and validating these intense emotions is vital; learning that anger and frustration are normal responses to unmet expectations is critical to navigating this period.

Gwinn and Hellman also explore how early life experiences impact an individual's capacity for hope. They use a tool, particularly Adverse Childhood Experiences (ACEs), to measure these experiences. Higher ACE scores often correlate with lower levels of hope, as these early traumas can profoundly affect one's worldview and sense of safety. Nevertheless, hope remains malleable, and individuals with high ACE scores can cultivate it through interventions, supportive relationships, and goal-oriented thinking. This resilience and ability to foster hope, even in the face of significant trauma, highlights the importance of empathy and nurturing hope during grieving (Gwinn & Hellman, 2022).

In grief, distinguishing between "present-oriented" and "future-oriented" hope is crucial. Present-oriented hope involves cherishing small joys and gratitude in the current moment, especially helpful when the future appears uncertain (Snyder et al., 2002). On the other hand, future-oriented hope is about setting goals and envisioning a life beyond current grief (Herth, 1991). This dual approach enables individuals to manage their immediate emotional needs while maintaining a sense of direction for the future.

Allowing the "survival window" with patience and grace for yourself and the impact of past traumas on hope is essential in the grieving process. It underscores the need for targeted support and intervention to foster hope, guiding individuals to rebuild a sense of purpose and direction in their lives (Gwinn & Hellman, 2022). As an active element in the grieving process, the dynamic nature of hope offers comfort and direction, manifesting through resilience and the support of others.

Navigating Loss: Suggestions & Support

Present-Oriented Hope

Present-oriented hope during grief focuses on finding and nurturing small, immediate sources of hope in the midst of the grieving process. Here are some examples:

Acknowledge and Accept Your Feelings: Recognize that having a wide range of emotions is okay. Accepting your feelings, whether sadness, anger, or confusion, is crucial in the healing process.

Mindful Appreciation of Simple Pleasures: Finding moments of peace or joy in everyday activities, like enjoying a cup of tea, walking in nature, or the warmth of sunlight.

Acknowledging Moments of Relief: Recognizing and being grateful for brief periods when grief feels lighter or more manageable, even if these moments are fleeting.

Set Realistic Expectations for Yourself: Understand that healing takes time. Be patient with yourself and recognize that it's okay to have good days and bad days.

Plan for Triggering Events: Holidays, anniversaries, and other significant dates can be challenging. Plan for these times by deciding how you want to spend the day and who you want to be with, and allowing flexibility to change these plans as needed.

Connecting with Loved Ones: Cherishing time spent with friends or family members who provide comfort, even if it's just a short conversation or shared silence.

Engaging in Comforting Routines: Maintaining or establishing daily routines that bring a sense of normalcy and stability, such as morning exercises, reading, or cooking.

Small Acts of Self-Care: Prioritizing self-care activities that offer immediate relief, such as taking a warm bath, listening to a favorite song undisturbed, or practicing deep breathing exercises.

Celebrate All Achievements: Acknowledging and celebrating small accomplishments, like completing a task or being able to express feelings through journaling or art.

Finding Solace in Memories: Experiencing moments of comfort when remembering positive memories of the loved one.

Practicing Gratitude: Actively noticing and being thankful for the good things still present in life, however small they may seem.

Nurturing Hope Through Creativity: Engaging in creative activities like painting, writing, or crafting can be therapeutic and provide a sense of accomplishment and expression.

Reflecting on Personal Growth: Recognizing personal growth and resilience developed through the grieving process, such as increased empathy, strength, or self-awareness.

These examples of present-oriented hope focus on the short term here and now, helping individuals in grief to find small pockets of hope and positivity in their daily lives. They serve as reminders that even during loss, moments of light and comfort can be found.

Future-Oriented Hope

Long-term, future-oriented hope is about looking forward and envisioning a life beyond the immediate grief. Here are some suggestions for cultivating this type of hope:

Setting Future Goals: Encourage setting small, achievable goals for the future. These can be as simple as planning a small trip, taking up a new hobby, or setting personal development goals. This helps in looking forward to something positive.

Visualizing a Positive Future: Practice visualization techniques where you imagine a future where you have adapted to the loss and found new meaning and joy in life. Visualization can help create a mental image of a hopeful future.

Building New Relationships and Strengthening Existing Ones: Invest time in building new relationships or deepening existing ones. Relationships can be a source of hope and provide a sense of connection and purpose.

Finding Meaning and Purpose: Engage in activities or causes that are meaningful to you. This could involve volunteering, mentoring others, or pursuing an important cause for your loved one.

Planning for Major Life Events: Start thinking about major future life events and how you can approach them in a way that honors your loss but also celebrates life. This might include family milestones, career advancements, or personal achievements.

Personal Growth and Learning: Consider pursuing new learning or personal development areas. This could be educational courses, learning new skills, or exploring new areas of interest.

Creating a Legacy: Think about ways to create a legacy in honor of your loved one. This could be through charitable work, a scholarship fund, or a community project.

Writing a Future Letter to Yourself: Write a letter to your future self, expressing hopes and dreams for the coming years. This can be a powerful way to articulate and affirm your hopes for the future.

Physical Health and Wellness: Focus on maintaining or improving your physical health. Physical well-being can significantly impact mental health and outlook on the future.

Mindfulness and Future-Oriented Meditation: Practice mindfulness and meditation techniques that focus on future positivity and resilience.

Seeking Professional Future Planning: For some, speaking with a life coach or counselor about future planning can be helpful. They can provide guidance in setting and achieving future-oriented goals.

Journaling Future Hopes and Dreams: Keep a journal where you regularly write down your hopes, dreams, and aspirations for the future. This can be a way to keep your future-oriented hope alive and evolving.

These suggestions aim to foster a sense of forward-looking hope, encouraging individuals to envision and work towards a future where they can find joy and fulfillment, even in the wake of loss.

Your ACE Score: A Conversation About Resilience and Hope

Acknowledging and discussing Adverse Childhood Experiences (ACEs) openly paves the way for more authentic conversations about our past, struggles, and the potential for hope and transformation. By bringing these experiences into the light, we begin dismantling the barriers of silence and stigma that often surround them.

Addressing the ACEs involves empathy and sensitivity. Recognizing the presence of trauma in our lives is not about assigning fault; it's about understanding its impact on our behaviors, feelings, and choices. This awareness can lead to meaningful change and restoration of power that trauma may have taken from us. It's essential to approach this topic with a non-judgmental attitude, acknowledging that everyone's experiences and responses to them are unique.

For many, learning about their ACE Score can be an eye-opening experience. It can explain specific patterns of behavior, emotional responses, and even health issues. Discussing these scores can help us see the link between past experiences and present challenges, creating a space for healing and growth. However, it's crucial to approach these conversations with care, avoiding any sense of blame or shame. The focus should be on learning, healing, and cultivating hope.

If you're interested in discovering your ACE Score, you can take a questionnaire from many health organizations online. This score can serve as a starting point for understanding your experiences and their long-term impacts. Remember, your ACE Score is not your destiny. It's a tool, a starting point for healing and building resilience. The conversation about hope and resilience begins here, where we acknowledge our past but look forward to a future where we take back our power from trauma. With the right support and resources, understanding your ACEs can be a transformative experience, allowing you to navigate the effects of past traumas and move toward a more hopeful and empowered future.

As someone deeply committed to supporting individuals through their experiences of trauma and grief, I offer guidance and empathy in navigating these complex and often challenging paths. My approach is grounded in trauma awareness, ensuring a safe and supportive environment where you can explore your past experiences at your own pace.

Together, we can delve into your ACE Score's insights and its implications in a compassionate and non-judgmental space. I can assist you in interpreting what this score means for you and how it might influence your current behaviors, relationships, and emotional well-being. More importantly, our sessions will focus on building resilience and hope, crafting a path that acknowledges your past and embraces a future filled with potential and growth.

If you feel ready to take this step and would like support in understanding your ACE Score and its impact, I invite you to contact me. My role is to be a partner in your healing journey, providing trauma-aware coaching that respects your unique experiences and fosters a sense of empowerment and hope. Together, we can work towards comprehending your past and reimagining and rebuilding a hopeful future.

In Closing

We sincerely hope that you have found solace and perhaps a newfound perspective on the multifaceted experience of grief. This book has been a tapestry woven with personal stories, research insights, and practical guidance, all aimed at illuminating the tapestry of loss and the surprising pathways to healing and growth it can reveal.

We've explored grief, which is not just a journey of pain and loss; it's also a profound teacher. It teaches us about the depths of love, the strength of the human spirit, and the resilience within each of us. We've seen how, in the heart of our darkest moments, a light of empathy, compassion, and a deeper appreciation for the fleeting beauty of life can emerge.

Remember, your journey through grief is uniquely your own. There is no right or wrong way to grieve, no set timeline for healing. What matters most is allowing yourself to feel, heal, and grow in your own time and in your own way. The stories and perspectives shared in this book are not just narratives; they are beacons of hope, reminding you that you are not alone in your journey.

We are forever changed but also forever connected to the vast tapestry of human experience. Carry this connection with you as you move forward, knowing that even in loss, there is a profound possibility for growth, love, and the discovery of unanticipated blessings.

Every day is an opportunity to remember that the journey through grief is not a path walked alone. We can rally around each other, and society can be taught. There is strength in the shared experiences and wisdom in these pages, and may they serve as a gentle reminder that there is still room for growth, love, and moments of unexpected joy amid your sorrow. Our stories are not just about loss but about living, learning, and transforming. In grief and healing, we find new ways to love, connect, and cherish life's preciousness.

As you close this book, we hope you carry the lessons learned and the comfort found within its pages. May you have the courage to face each day with an open heart, ready to embrace life's fullness, and move forward with a renewed sense of purpose and joy.

Bibliography

Ader, R., & Cohen, N. (1993). Psychoneuroimmunology: Conditioning and stress. *Annual Review of Psychology, 44*, 53–85.

Bonanno, G. A. (2004). Loss, trauma, and human resilience: Have we underestimated the human capacity to thrive after extremely aversive events? *American Psychologist, 59*(1), 20–28.

Bonanno, G. A. (2009). The Other Side of Sadness: What the New Science of Bereavement Tells Us About Life After Loss. Basic Books.

Boss, P. (1999). Ambiguous loss: Learning to live with unresolved grief. Harvard University Press.

Bradberry, T., & Greaves, J. (2009). *Emotional Intelligence 2.0.* TalentSmart.

Carter, J. (2004). *Nasty People.* McGraw-Hill.

Center of Complicated Grief, Columbia University. (2018). Complicated Grief. Retrieved from https://complicatedgrief.columbia.edu/

Crenshaw, D. A. (2007). Bereavement: Counseling the grieving throughout the life cycle. Continuum.

David, S. (2016). Emotional Agility: Get Unstuck, Embrace Change, and Thrive in Work and Life. Penguin Books.

Doka, K. J., & Martin, T. L. (2010). Grieving beyond gender: Understanding the ways men and women mourn. Routledge.

Enright, R. D. (2001). Forgiveness is a choice: A step-by-step process for resolving anger and restoring hope. American Psychological Association.

Fell, L. C., Beltz, E. G., Elizabeth, A., Martin, D. L., Rollins, M., & Kelly, R. G. (2015). *Grief Diaries: Surviving Loss of a Child*. AlyBlue Media.

Fisher, J. (2017). Healing the fragmented selves of trauma survivors: Overcoming internal self-alienation. Routledge.

Frankl, V. E. (2006). *Man's Search for Meaning*. Beacon Press. (Original work published 1946)

Fredrickson, B. L. (2001). The role of positive emotions in positive psychology: The broaden-and-build theory of positive emotions. *American Psychologist, 56*(3), 218–226.

Gibson, L. C. (2015). Adult Children of Emotionally Immature Parents: How to Heal from Distant, Rejecting, or Self-Involved Parents. New Harbinger Publications, Inc.

Gibson, L. C. (2019). Recovering from Emotionally Immature Parents: Practical Tools to Establish Boundaries and Reclaim Your Emotional Autonomy. New Harbinger Publications, Inc.

Gilat, I., & Shahar, G. (2007). Emotional first aid for a suicide crisis: Comparison between telephonic hotline and internet. *Psychiatry, 70*(1), 12–18.

Green, A., Brown, B., & Clark, C. (2018). Empathy and resilience: Understanding the intersection. *Journal of Marital and Family Therapy, 44*(2), 345–360.

Greene, J. (2018). *Emotional Intelligence*. Jacob Greene.

Gwinn, C., & Hellman, C. (2022). *HOPE Rising: How the Science of HOPE Can Change Your Life*. Morgan James Publishing.

Harvard Health Publishing. (n.d.). Grief can hurt in more ways than one. *Harvard Health Blog*. Retrieved from https://www.health.harvard.edu/mind-and-mood/grief-can-hurt-in-more-ways-than-one

Harvard Health Publishing. (2019). Coping with grief and loss during the holidays. Retrieved from https://www.health.harvard.edu

Hayes, S. C., & Wilson, K. G. (2021). Acceptance and Commitment Therapy for Unresolved Grief: Fostering Acceptance and Value-Driven Behavior. *Journal of Contextual Behavioral Science, 19*(2), 134–143.

Hayes, S., & Smith, M. (2022). Acceptance and Commitment Therapy for Grief and Loss. *Journal of Contemporary Psychotherapy, 40*(3), 159–168.

Herth, K. (1991). Development and refinement of an instrument to measure hope. *Scholarly Inquiry for Nursing Practice, 5*(1), 39–51.

Hooyman, N. R., & Kramer, B. J. (2006). *Living through loss: Interventions across the life span*. Columbia University Press.

Johnson, A., & Smith, B. (2021). Unfinished Business: Understanding Guilt and Regret in Grief. *Journal of Bereavement Therapy, 35*(2), 102–115.

Kessler, D. (2005). On grief and grieving: Finding the meaning of grief through the five stages of loss. Simon & Schuster.

Kessler, D. (2019). Finding Meaning: The Sixth Stage of Grief. Scribner.

Klass, D., & Walter, T. (2001). Processes of grieving: How bonds are continued. In M. S. Stroebe, R. O. Hansson, W. Stroebe, & H. Schut (Eds.), *Handbook of Bereavement Research: Consequences, Coping, and Care* (pp. 431–448). American Psychological Association.

Koenig, H. G. (2007). Religion and Remedy: How Different Religions View Health and Sickness. Oxford University Press.

Kübler-Ross, E. (1969). *On death and dying*. Macmillan.

Kübler-Ross, E., & Kessler, D. (2005). On Grief and Grieving: Finding the Meaning of Grief Through the Five Stages of Loss. Simon & Schuster.

Levine, P. A. (2015). Trauma and Memory: Brain and Body in a Search for the Living Past. North Atlantic Books.

Lee, C., & Brown, S. (2018). Mindfulness and Acceptance in Grieving: Clinical Applications. *Mindfulness Research Review, 12*(1), 76–85.

Lee, C. (2019). The role of empathy in grieving couples. *Couples Therapy Journal, 10*(1), 24–35.

MacKenzie, J. (2019). Whole Again: Healing Your Heart and Rediscovering Your True Self After Toxic Relationships. Penguin Random House LLC.

Martinez, R., & Thompson, H. (2021). Building resilience in relationships after loss. *American Journal of Family Psychology, 29*(4), 541–556.

McLaren, K. (2010). The Language of Emotions: What Your Feelings Are Trying to Tell You. Sounds True.

Monfils, M. H., & Holmes, E. A. (2018). Memory consolidation, reconsolidation, and extinction. In J. H. Byrne (Ed.), *Learning and memory: A comprehensive reference* (2nd ed., Vol. 3, pp. 227–244). Academic Press.

Neimeyer, R. A. (2001). *Meaning Reconstruction & the Experience of Loss*. American Psychological Association.

Neimeyer, R. A. (2001). Reauthoring life narratives: Grief therapy as meaning reconstruction. *The Israel Journal of Psychiatry and Related Sciences, 38*(3-4), 171–183.

Neimeyer, R. A. (2006). Techniques of Grief Therapy: Creative Practices for Counseling the Bereaved. Routledge.

Nolan, R. (2021). Stoicism: A Complete Guide to Empower Your Mindset and Timeless Wisdom to Gain Emotional Resilience, Confidence and Calmness. Gianpiero Oliva.

Patel, S., & Kumar, V. (2022). Transformation through grief: How couples find new connections. *Journal of Grief and Loss, 31*(3), 112–128.

Pargament, K. I. (1997). The Psychology of Religion and Coping: Theory, Research, Practice. The Guilford Press.

Parkes, C. M. (1972). *Bereavement: Studies of grief in adult life*. International Universities Press.

Parkes, C. M. (1998). Bereavement: Studies of Grief in Adult Life. Routledge.

Parnell, L. (2013). Attachment-focused EMDR: Healing relational trauma. W. W. Norton & Company.

Porges, S. W. (2011). The Polyvagal Theory: Neurophysiological Foundations of Emotions, Attachment, Communication, and Self-regulation. Norton & Company.

Rando, T. A. (1986). Grief, Dying, and Death: Clinical Interventions for Caregivers. Research Press.

Rando, T. A. (1988). How to go on living when someone you love dies. Bantam Books.

Rando, T. A. (1993). *Treatment of Complicated Mourning*. Champaign, IL: Research Press.

Rogers, C. R., & Farson, R. E. (1957). *Active listening*. Chicago: University of Chicago Industrial Relations Center.

Rogers, M. L., Floyd, F. J., Mailick, M. R., Greenberg, J., & Hong, J. (2008). Long-term effects of the death of a child on parents' adjustment in midlife. *Journal of Family Psychology, 22*(2), 203–211. https://doi.org/10.1037/0893-3200.22.2.203

Ruiz, D. M. (1997). The Four Agreements: A Practical Guide to Personal Freedom (A Toltec Wisdom Book). Amber-Allen Publishing.

Schwartz, R. C. (2001). *Internal Family Systems Therapy*. The Guilford Press.

Shear, M. K. (2015). Complicated grief. *New England Journal of Medicine, 372*, 153–160.

Silk, S., & Goldman, B. (2013, April 7). How not to say the wrong thing. *Los Angeles Times*. Retrieved from https://www.latimes.com

Silverman, P. R. (1999). Helping children cope with the loss of a loved one: A guide for grownups. Free Spirit Publishing.

Smith, L., & Cook, A. (2019). Practical support in bereavement: An empirical study. *Journal of Loss and Trauma, 24*(4), 350–362. https://doi.org/10.1080/15325024.2019.1587974

Smith, J., & Johnson, L. (2020). Communication in times of grief. *Journal of Couple Relations, 15*(2), 89–104.

Snyder, C. R. (2002). Hope Theory: Rainbows in the Mind. *Psychological Inquiry, 13*(4), 249–275.

Stroebe, M. S., & Schut, H. (1999). The Dual Process Model of Coping with Bereavement: Rationale and Description. *Death Studies, 23*(3), 197–224.

Stroebe, M., Schut, H., & Stroebe, W. (2005). Attachment in coping with bereavement: A theoretical integration. *Review of General Psychology, 9*(1), 48–66.

Stroebe, M., Schut, H., & Stroebe, W. (2007). Health outcomes of bereavement. *The Lancet, 370*(9603), 1960–1973. https://doi.org/10.1016/S0140-6736(07)61816-9

Taylor, J. B. (2021). Whole brain living: The anatomy of choice and the four characters that drive our life. Hay House, Inc.

Thompson, H., Greene, M., & Roberts, N. (2019). The Healing Power of Self-Forgiveness in Grief. *The American Journal of Grief Counseling, 18*(3), 300–318.

van der Kolk, B. A. (2014). The Body Keeps the Score: Brain, Mind, and Body in the Healing of Trauma. Penguin Books.

Wagner, E., & White, G. (2021). Shared experiences in couple's grief: A path to healing. *Journal of Relationship Therapy, 17*(3), 201–218.

Willcox, G. (1982). *Feelings: Converting Negatives to Positives*. Center for Application of Psychological Type.

Williams, R., & Martinez, L. (2020). Cognitive Behavioral Techniques for Grief: A Practical Approach. *Journal of Cognitive Psychotherapy, 28*(4), 234–249.

Wolfelt, A. D. (2003). Companioning the bereaved: A soulful guide for caregivers. Companion Press.

Worden, J. W. (1996). *Children and grief: When a parent dies*. Guilford Press.

Worden, J. W. (2009). Grief Counseling and Grief Therapy: A Handbook for the Mental Health Practitioner (4th ed.). Springer Publishing Company.

Zisook, S., & Shear, K. (2009). Grief and bereavement: What psychiatrists need to know. *World Psychiatry, 8*(2), 67–74. https://doi.org/10.1002/j.2051-5545.2009.tb00217.x

About the Authors

Kathy and Peter George, along with their surviving children, make their home in the scenic landscapes of Tennessee. Their lives took a transformative turn with the loss of their six-year-old son, Trevor, to Sudden Unexplained Death in Childhood (SUDC), an experience that profoundly shaped their approach to grief and healing.

Kathy, MS, CMHC, is the Founder of Reclaiming Hope Coach and a Trauma-Competent Grief Coach. Her understanding of loss was further deepened by her own battle with breast cancer. These experiences inspired her to pursue a Master's in Clinical Mental Health Counseling. Certified in grief education, hypnosis, and as a Quantum Alignment System Practitioner, she integrates clinical expertise with holistic approaches to guide others through their healing journeys.

Peter brings his project management background and personal grief journey to support other fathers navigating the loss of a child. His organizational and leadership abilities, combined with his firsthand understanding of parental grief, allow him to offer unique insights and peer support to families facing similar challenges.

Together, Kathy and Peter find solace in nature and the vibrant energy of live music near their Tennessee home. Through their writing and individual work, they create spaces where grief is acknowledged and understood. Their shared mission stems from their own story of loss: helping others find hope and healing on their unique paths forward.

For those seeking guidance through grief, Kathy offers virtual coaching services worldwide. Learn more at reclaiminghopecoach.com.

"You are not alone in your grief. Join us on this path of healing, resilience, and hope. Begin your journey today."

www.ingramcontent.com/pod-product-compliance
Lightning Source LLC
Chambersburg PA
CBHW070918120626
46546CB00001B/312